Happiness is like a butterfly which, when pursued, is always beyond our grasp, but, if you will sit down quietly, may alight upon you.

—Nathaniel Hawthorne

Butterflies

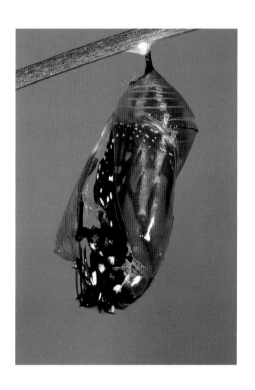

Text by David Badger
Photography by Brian Kenney

CRESTLINE

This edition published in 2010 by
CRESTLINE
A division of BOOK SALES, INC.
276 Fifth Avenue Suite 206
New York, New York 10001
USA

First published in 2006 by Voyageur Press, an imprint
of MBI Publishing Company, Galtier Plaza, Suite 200,
380 Jackson Street, St. Paul, MN 55101-3885 USA

Library of Congress Cataloging-in-Publication Data

Badger, David P.
  Butterflies / text by David Badger ; photography by
Brian Kenney.
    p. cm.
  Includes bibliographical references and index.
  ISBN-13: 978-0-7858-2690-3
  ISBN-10: 0-7858-2690-4
  1. Butterflies. 2. Butterflies--Pictorial works. I.
Kenney, Brian. II. Title.
  QL542.B33 2006
  595.78'9--dc22

                                    2006015616

Edited by Danielle J. Ibister
Designed by Jennifer Bergstrom

Printed in China

On the front cover: Eastern tiger swallowtail

On the back cover: Malachite (bottom right); giant swallowtail (bottom left); Southern dogface (top left); monarch (top right).

On the spine: Black swallowtail newly emerged from chrysalis

On the endpapers: Queen butterfly wing detail

On the frontispiece: Pair of American painted lady butterflies (*Vanessa virginiensis*) showing pink flash colors on underwings.

On the title page: Monarch butterflies (*Danaus plexippus*) overwintering at El Rosario Butterfly Sanctuary, north of Zitácuaro, Mexico.

On the title page inset: Monarch butterfly emerges from its chrysalis.

On the Table of Contents: Detail of wing pattern on the underside of a red-spotted purple butterfly (*Limenitis arthemis*).

Eastern black swallowtail recently emerged from its chrysalis dries its wings. (Top)

Two monarch caterpillars feed on a milkweed hostplant. (Bottom)

Facing page: A large tree nymph (*Idea leuconoe*) in flight.

Eastern black swallowtails

Eastern black swallowtails (*Papilio polyxenes*) exhibit sexual dimorphism. The female (on left) has more black and increased blue spotting on its hind-wings; the male (right) has a broader band of yellow.

Dedication

For Ross Arthur Taggart
1921–2005
Friend, photographer, and father-in-law
extraordinaire.

—*David Badger*

For my parents,
Allan and Ruth Kenney,
Who encouraged me to follow my dreams.

—*Brian Kenney*

Acknowledgments

The author and photographer wish to express their gratitude to a number of individuals for their assistance with this book. The author is especially indebted to Dr. Marc Minno, entomologist, ecologist, and author, for reviewing the entire manuscript and offering countless invaluable suggestions. Author-naturalist Rita Venable, president of the Middle Tennessee Chapter of the North American Butterfly Association (NABA) and recent editor of *Butterfly Gardening*, organized field trips and introduced the author to the wrangling and temporary lodging of larvae; Nancy Garden and other chapter members offered encouragement and fellowship. Dr. Frank Hale, University of Tennessee entomologist, provided indispensable resources, and Dr. Robert Anderson, professor of entomology at Idaho State University, fielded inquiries about Western butterflies. Laura Halverson, collection care assistant at the San Diego Natural History Museum, graciously opened drawer after drawer in the entomology collection and discussed their contents. Also helpful was the staff at the Cecil B. Day Butterfly Center at Callaway Gardens (Pine Mountain, Georgia).

The author would also like to thank Michael Dregni, Voyageur Press publisher, for his patience and support with this project; Danielle Ibister, for her deft editing of the manuscript; ever-supportive colleague Ray Wong for the eleventh-hour mug shot; and photographer-collaborator Brian Kenney, who initiated this project, for his unfailing encouragement, assistance, and resilience. Special thanks to my wife, Sherry, and son, Jeff, for their remarkable forbearance and genuine enthusiasm for this undertaking. And a nod to Katie the Miracle Dog, who survived two spinal surgeries and kept vigil on the couch beside the laptop throughout nearly the entire enterprise.

Marc Minno helped the photographer find the elusive harvester butterfly just when he had come to the conclusion that it was only a myth. Joyce "The Caterpillar Hunter" Sprenger, Ruth Linsley, Bill Boothe, Fred Santana, Pete Carmichael, John Pontier, Jacqueline Miller (Allyn Museum), Debbie Hill, Tim Adams, Buck and Linda Cooper, Terry Powell, and the members of the Sarasota, Florida, chapter of NABA shared natural history observations and provided field assistance. Butterfly World (Coconut Creek, Florida), Cypress Gardens (Winter Haven, Florida), Butterfly Rainforest (Gainesville, Florida), and Magic Wings Butterfly House and Insectarium (Durham, North Carolina) generously allowed the photographer to take pictures in their conservatories. The photographer is particularly indebted to Richard Hesterberg for his expert help in identifying some of the more difficult species and unusual behaviors.

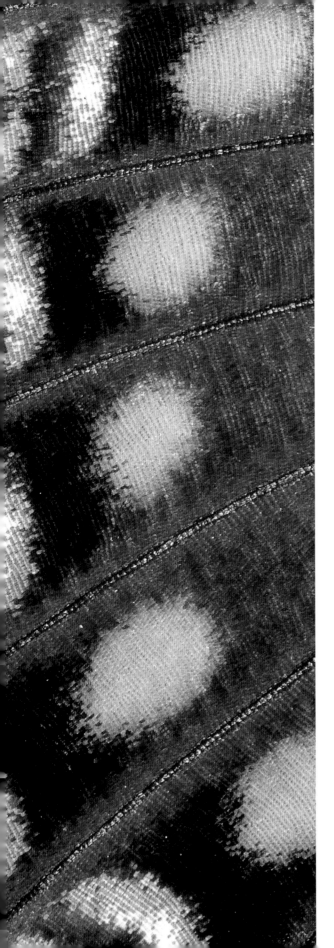

Contents

Introduction

When I was growing up on the North Shore of Chicago, I used to chase butterflies in my mother's garden. Armed with a cheesecloth net, I would stalk swallowtails and monarchs among the flowers and shrubs, deliberately snubbing the more humdrum cabbage butterflies, and take a swipe at the occasional mourning cloak basking in the sun. Exotic-looking caterpillars and gleaming green-and-gold "cocoons" (or, more properly, "chrysalides") often appeared as if by magic on milkweeds in a vacant lot adjoining a side alley. Then one day I caught a smooth green snake in that alley—and neglected butterflies for the next forty years.

Today, after writing several books for Voyageur Press about snakes, frogs, and lizards, I have found my way back to the butterflies of my youth (or, more accurately, a talented and persuasive photographer from Florida found me). The result is a collaboration that showcases Brian Kenney's striking color images of butterflies from around the world, flanked by species accounts and supporting text about physical characteristics and behavior, butterfly-human relations, conservation, and photography. By no means a technical volume or field guide, this work is intended for butterfly enthusiasts and anyone else who cherishes the splendors of the natural world.

Who knew—besides the several million people who regularly visit butterfly conservatories, zoos, museums, municipal gardens, state and national parks, entomology (insect) websites, and libraries with large sections devoted to natural history—that butterflies could be so mesmerizing? Practically every sunlit day that I commute to work on a two-lane highway through pastures, fields, and woodlands (and mushrooming residential developments) south of Nashville, Tennessee, I have "close encounters" with butterflies that flap in the general direction of my windshield. But until I was invited to collaborate on this book, I paid them little attention. Now I crane my neck to differentiate fritillaries from monarchs, black swallowtails from red-spotted purples, and painted ladies from buckeyes. Increasingly, I get them right.

While butterflies may not boast the inexplicable seductiveness of serpents, the dangerous allure of giant "man-eating" monitor lizards, or the quirky appeal of dart-poison frogs, they do inspire universal affection. Butterflies' vibrant colors and dizzying patterns often startle and wow the beholder. Even the "smallest, plainest ones," declares ecologist Robert Michael Pyle, "offer brilliance and beauty quite up to that of the tropical dazzlers."

Tawny emperor
A tawny emperor butterfly (*Asterocampa clyton*) pauses on lantana, displaying the mottled underside of its wings.

> *The butterfly counts not months*
> *but moments*
> *and has time enough.*
>
> —Rabindramath Tagore
> quoted in *The Spirit of Butterflies*

In 2005, entomologists David Grimaldi and Michael S. Engle reported there were about 14,500 described species of "true butterflies" and another 3,500 species of skippers—a total of some 18,000 species worldwide. For centuries, moths were lumped together with butterflies, but today, scientists differentiate between the two (butterflies comprise just 13 percent of the order Lepidoptera, while the rest are moths). Their chief differences are physical and behavioral: butterflies have knobbed or club-tipped antennae, while moths generally have tapered or feather-shaped antennae; moths have hairy bodies, while most butterflies have smooth, thin ones; butterflies are typically brightly colored, while most moths are not; butterflies generally bask in the sun with their wings spread open but rest with their wings closed over their back, while moths commonly rest with their wings spread flat or closed at an angle; almost all butterflies are diurnal (day-active), while most moths are nocturnal.

Zebra swallowtail
A zebra swallowtail (*Eurytides marcellus*) rests on bougainvillea flowers.

The word "butterfly" apparently derives from the Old English *buterfloege* or *butterfleoge*, perhaps because of a superstition during the Middle Ages that fairies masqueraded as these flying insects to steal butter. Another explanation suggests that the name refers to the brimstone (*Gonepteryx rhamni*), a common yellow species once called the "butter-colored fly." The French word for butterfly, *papillon*, is preserved in the English word "pavilion" (a tent with flaps that can be raised like butterfly wings) and has evolved into the French slang term for "parking ticket," a yellow slip of paper that frequently flaps in the wind. Another root source for "butterfly" may be the Dutch *boterschijte*, a reference to the color of the insect's excrement.

Whatever the etymological origin of the name, entomologists believe these insects evolved some 100 to 144 million years ago. Only about fifty butterfly fossils have ever been found, however, because their bodies were so soft and their wings so fragile. Among the oldest are discoveries estimated to be 50 to 70 million years old from Colorado's Green River shales and Florissant Fossil Beds National Monument.

Over the centuries, common names bestowed upon butterflies have come to include some distinct oddities. There are satyrs, wood nymphs, painted ladies, shoemakers, snouts, hairstreaks, crackers, daggerwings, admirals, and viceroys. Even more eccentrically named are the postman, striped policeman, common sailor, gaudy commodore, swarthy skipper, pirate butterfly, common Jezebel, brown playboy, Himalayan jester, hermit, wizard, wanderer, dogface, hoary comma, and

big greasy butterfly. Sly scientific names have been coined as well, including tributes to entomologist-author Vladimir Nabokov and his fictional characters—e.g., Peru's *Madeleinea lolita*, Argentina's *Pseudolucia humbert*, and Chile's *Nabokovia ada*—and to bug-loving "Far Side" cartoonist Gary Larson (*Serratoterga larsoni*, an Ecuadorian rain forest butterfly).

In truth, butterflies have held an attraction for men, women, and children since time immemorial. Poets, painters, playwrights, novelists, photographers, dancers, musicians, designers, craftspeople—artists of every stripe—have been inspired by the beauty and grace of butterflies. Scientists, engineers, and entrepreneurs have studied the aerodynamics of butterfly flight, the role of biological clocks and polarized-light receptors in migration, the physiological components of thermoregulation and hibernation, the chemical processes of metamorphosis, the structural color principles of iridescent wing scales, and the phenomenon of compound eyes.

Explorers once lusted after exotic specimens for private collections and public museums; today, preserved and phony specimens are sold on the Internet, many to languish in drawers as "investments," others to embellish walls. Live butterflies are big business, too, shipped from butterfly farms as adults in glassine envelopes for release at weddings, or as pupae for biology classes to observe when they emerge from their mummylike sacs. The many butterfly conservatories around the world are by far the most important market for farm-raised chrysalides today, offering visitors an opportunity to glimpse exotic species as they are truly meant to be seen—alive and in flight.

American painted lady

An American painted lady (*Vanessa virginiensis*), named after the well-rouged streetwalkers of London and brightly painted Victorian-style homes on the streets of San Francisco, offers a glimpse of the elaborate patterns on the underside of her wings.

Whether incarcerated or in the wild, most adult butterflies do not live long. The average lifespan is measured in days and rarely exceeds a week or two. Nonetheless, some species live a bit longer, others overwinter as adults, and *Heliconius* longwings, fortified by amino acids they consume in pollen, have been known to survive up to nine months. Members of this long-lived genus are also recognized for their exceptional memories. "They remember favorite flowers" and roosting sites, reports naturalist Sharman Apt Russell,

and "they remember to hold a grudge, avoiding spots where some scientist captured them days earlier."

Butterfly enthusiasts in eighteenth- and nineteenth-century England amassed (and occasionally stole) huge collections, built private conservatories, joined societies, and transacted their business at London's Swan Tavern. In 1845, one rash collector declared he was "on the look-out for an entomological wife...one that will be useful as well as ornamental." A century later, the first two men to run the mile in less than four minutes trained by chasing butterflies—and one went on to become a distinguished lepidopterist (butterfly expert).

In America, patrons and politicians commissioned westward explorers to bring back new specimens; one unlucky collector lost his butterflies when his pack-train drivers dumped the insects at night to guzzle the alcohol in which they were preserved. Alcohol entices butterflies, too: California sisters (*Adelpha bredowii*) and buckeyes (*Junonia coenia*) have been known to "tipple immoderately" at wineries in Napa Valley, says Pyle, and red admirals (*Vanessa atalanta*) that consume quantities of fermented fruit sugars can become inebriated.

Observers of butterflies habitually wax ecstatic. Among them, the American poet Walt Whitman, photographed for the Library of Congress holding a butterfly apparently made of cardboard, gushed over a swarm of these "beautiful, spiritual insects" that he spied on a path "holding a revel, a gyration-dance, or butterfly good-time." The painter James McNeill Whistler, nicknamed "Butterfly" by his mother, incorporated a butterfly design into his signature; Winslow Homer and Pablo Picasso painted butterflies, and Andy Warhol printed lithographs of an endangered species. Shortly before World War I, young German naturalists flocked to France to sketch wing patterns of native butterflies; suspicious residents, spotting errors in the drawings, exposed the Germans as spies encrypting maps into their designs.

One present-day admirer of monarch butterflies, the Mexican pilot Francisco "Vico" Gutierrez, constructed an ultralight motorized glider, painted it like a monarch, and set out with a crew in August 2005 to follow the monarchs' migration from Quebec, Canada, to the forests of Michoacán, Mexico. His objective was to call attention to the plight of monarchs today and to produce a documentary "from their point of view."

Around the world, avid "butterfliers" lure migrating and resident species to their gardens with nectar plants and larval hostplants. Some take field trips and ecotours sponsored by environmental groups, participate in North American Butterfly Association (NABA) Fourth of July butterfly counts, and tag butterflies for Monarch Watch, the Monarch Monitoring Project, and the Young Entomologists' Society. Many flock to observation points such as Cape May, New Jersey, in September to watch monarchs migrating southward along the Atlantic flyway. Every fall, New Orleanians drive across Lake Pontchartrain's twenty-four–mile causeway to behold streams of monarchs migrating to Mexico; post–Hurricane Katrina, the vantage point may change, but the showy procession of Mardi Gras–garbed monarchs will continue. Seasonal explosions of sulphur butterflies that wing through Gainesville, Florida, and painted ladies that swarm across California and the Southwest—some at speeds of twenty-five miles per hour—often hit humans head-on. In the spring of 2005, painted ladies collided with San Diego lifeguards, surfers, cyclists, and pedestrians and left gooey yellow splatters on windshields and highways.

Butterflies can be in your face, on your vehicle, or on the tip of your tongue: anxious people have "butterflies in the stomach"; social butterflies flit from party to party; swimmers compete in the butterfly stroke;

the "butterfly-brained" are intellectual light-weights; and assorted butterfly fish, snails, screws, valves, chairs, bombs, bushes, tulips, kisses, and other marvels await us in life.

There are, I recognize, already many volumes about this variety of insect. But, having worked previously with one gifted photographer (the late John Netherton) and now with another (Brian Kenney), both of whom convinced me to join their book projects by demonstrating their artistry with a lens, I firmly believe their photographs merit wide-ranging audiences. While most of my own research has been of the library sort, I have also decamped to conservatories and vivaria at Callaway Gardens, Georgia, and in the Nashville area; joined several NABA-sponsored field trips and butterfly counts; and examined the remarkable collection of specimens pinned in archival foam and stored in wooden drawers inside humidity- and temperature-controlled cases at the San Diego Natural History Museum.

On a recent trip to Glacier National Park with my family, we observed checkerspots and other northern Rocky Mountains butterflies at high elevations and, while whitewater rafting on the Flathead River, encountered numerous Western tiger swallowtails (*Papilio rutulus*) that swooped down to inspect our raft. When I asked entomology professor Robert Anderson of Idaho State University if the swallowtails might have perceived our yellow raft or red lifejackets as a giant nectar source, he offered an alternative hypothesis: perhaps our "large spot of yellow" resembled a concentration of tiger swallowtails, which often "mud-puddle" by the hundreds beside rivers and lakes to imbibe mineral-rich fluids.

Over a series of three summers, I collected caterpillars from a nearby meadow—Gulf and variegated fritillaries, buckeyes, and monarchs—and watched them metamorphose from small larval houseguests (gourmands all, gorging on fresh passionflower leaves, butter-and-eggs, or milkweed) into dashingly handsome, fragile yet sturdy adults. Their stages were fascinating to watch at close range: day-by-day growth of the caterpillars, periodic molts, chrysalis formation, resting, splitting of the pupal shell, emergence of the adult, secretion of meconium, and hardening of the wings. Then the inevitable sendoff—and Godspeed!

Researching and writing this book has been a real education, and perhaps readers will find it an education, too. But, more important, I hope they find the *butterflies* interesting. As the great evolutionary biologist (and eloquent entomologist) Edward O. Wilson once declared: "Mysterious and little-known organisms still live within reach of where you sit. Splendor awaits in minute proportions." They're all around us; all we have to do is open our eyes.

Cabbage white butterflies
Cabbage white butterflies (*Pieris rapae*) first arrived in Canada in 1860, reportedly as larval stowaways aboard ships from Europe. Today, they are found across the entire continental United States.

Chapter 1
Butterflies and People

In the spring of 1939, shortly before aerial bombs began their rain of destruction on London and the English countryside, a former British Royal Army soldier paid a visit to a butterfly farm in Kent. During a tour of the breeding grounds, the butterfly farmer's son later recalled, the visitor reminisced about his days as a prisoner of war in South Africa during the Boer War and said he "used to while away the time watching butterflies" when he exercised in the prison compound. Now the former fighter yearned to stock the grounds of his country home with butterflies.

But before a promised invitation to the visitor's home could take place, communication abruptly broke off. Winston Churchill was named first lord of the admiralty and summoned to Whitehall. Only after World War II and his decisive term as prime minister was Churchill finally able to stock his beloved Chartwell with red admirals, swallowtails, black-veined whites, vanessas, peacocks, tortoiseshells, and other butterflies. He took great pleasure, he later explained, in sitting for hours in his butterfly house, watching butterflies emerge from their chrysalides and setting these tiny detainees free.

Sir Winston wasn't the only world leader captivated by butterflies. Some five thousand years earlier, Egyptian pharaohs were laid to rest in tombs adorned with paintings of butterflies, which symbolized their presence in the afterlife; similarly, imperial Romans and Greeks believed butterflies represented the souls of the deceased. In the New World, Aztecs of high social rank carried bouquets of flowers but declined to smell their tips, reserving them for butterflies—reincarnations of warriors who died in battle. In North America, Chief Sitting Bull of the Sioux nation reportedly wore a monarch affixed to his ceremonial headdress and, in a famous portrait, sports a monarch in the band of his felt hat.

Around the world, diverse cultures have spun numerous myths and folktales about butterflies, many sharing key elements and motifs. The Greeks gave the butterfly the name *psyche*, which means "soul"; unearthed Greek coins, beads, and funeral monuments depict images of butterflies and chrysalides. Roman storytellers told of Cupid, the god of love, and Psyche, a gorgeous mortal whom Cupid's jealous mother, Venus, instructed him to stay away from. But Cupid fell in love with Psyche, and eventually his father, Jupiter, was obliged to intervene, bestowing immortality upon Psyche so that she might marry his heartsick son.

Associations of butterflies with immortality and souls of the dead are legion, transcending

Malachite
A malachite butterfly (*Siproeta stelenes*) sleeps upside down on a milkweed stem. Early-morning dew is visible on the underside of its wings.

Butterflies add another dimension to the garden, for they are like dream flowers— childhood dreams—which have broken loose from their stalks and escaped into the sunshine. Air and angels. This is the way I look upon their presence, not as a professional entomologist.

—Miriam Rothschild

Migration sign
Monarch butterfly migration is important to tourism in parts of Mexico. This sign in Michoacán, near one of the monarchs' winter colonies, reads: "Driver: Protect the monarch butterfly. Slow your speed."

classical mythology and appearing in European and Asian legends as well. One Spanish custom requires an heir to cast wine over a deceased person's ashes, writes author-artist Maraleen Manos-Jones, "as a toast to the butterfly that will escape with the soul." That explains the region's popular epitaph: "My butterfly flies inebriated." In Ireland, a seventeenth-century law forbade the killing of white butterflies because they might be the souls of children; in Wales and Germany, citizens believed the soul left the body in the form of a white butterfly. Black butterflies are a grim omen in Mexico, the Dominican Republic, and Haiti, portending death or bad luck for the occupant of a house where a butterfly lands on the front door. In the Philippines, newspapers reported that a black butterfly was seen entering the palace of President Ferdinand Marcos just prior to his death. In Indonesia, a butterfly that enters a house is believed to be the spirit of a deceased relative and must not be killed. In Samoa, catching a butterfly can have fateful consequences: the spirit of the butterfly may in turn deprive its captor of life or personal liberty.

Yet in Asia a pair of butterflies can symbolize everlasting love and happiness, and guests bring silk or paper butterflies to weddings as a blessing to the couple. In China, a Ming emperor once released butterflies in the presence of beautiful young women to choose his "true love," and in Japan, an emperor set butterflies free at garden parties to land on maidens who then received royal "favors." In Africa, butterflies are associated with medicinal properties: Nigerian bachelors are sometimes instructed to bathe with soap made from swallowtails to attract a bride, and young men from the Ivory Coast rub colorful scales from butterfly wings onto their bodies to grow pubic hair and enhance their virility.

Native Americans called butterflies "flying flowers," and many regarded them as messengers who carried human wishes aloft to the Great Spirit. According to Blackfoot tradition, butterflies brought dreams to sleeping adults and children, and the Zuni believed butterflies could predict weather. Navajo men and boys sometimes rubbed wing scales onto their legs before a race to confer light-footedness and speed. Early residents of the Ozarks and Appalachians spun legends about fritillaries: Count the number of large silver spots on the underside of a fritillary's wings, and that amount in silver dollars would soon come your way.

The relationship between humans and butterflies, of course, does not consist entirely of superstitions and myths. While a few butterfly species may be agricultural pests, humans have long coveted butterflies for their extraordinary beauty and exhibited exotic specimens in conservatories and private collections to observe the insects alive. One of the Victorian era's most remarkable lepidopterists was a woman named Margaret Fountaine, who at the age of twenty-nine began photographing, sketching, and painting butterflies from Italy and Tibet to South Africa and Jamaica. After her death in Trinidad at age seventy-eight, her collection of 22,000 butterflies was bequeathed to a museum in Norwich, England. Fountaine's passion for butterflies placed her in the company of many other artists, including

Albrecht Dürer, William Blake, Vincent van Gogh, Edmund Dulac, and M. C. Escher, whose butterfly works are displayed in museums and private collections. Architect-designer Frank Lloyd Wright's celebrated butterfly stained-glass window and lamp are exhibited in the Susan Lawrence Dana House in Illinois, and innumerable pieces of jewelry, enamel, china, clothing, quilts, and furniture have featured butterflies in other designers' works.

Butterflies are evident everywhere you look. Composers write operas ("Madame Butterfly") and songs ("Poor Butterfly") about them, musicians name their groups after them (Iron Butterfly), and singer Janis Joplin painted psychedelic butterflies on her Volkswagen. Children's books open the eyes of youngsters to the wonders of caterpillars and butterflies, while writers such as John Nichols (author of the gonzo environmental screed *The Voice of the Butterfly*) incorporate these creatures into their fiction. John Steinbeck devoted an entire chapter of *Sweet Thursday*, his sequel to *Cannery Row*, to peculiar events at the annual monarch festival in Pacific Grove, California, and poets such as Alexander Pope, William Wordsworth, John Keats, Emily Dickinson, D. H. Lawrence, and Robert Frost have written odes to these insects.

Moviemakers too have incorporated butterflies in their work. *Butterflies Are Free* borrows its title from a line by Charles Dickens; *Papillon* tells the true-life tale of a convict (played by Steve McQueen) with a butterfly tattoo and a knack for escaping from prison on Devil's Island. More recently, Philippe Muyl's *The Butterfly* tells the story of an aging lepidopterist whose quest for a

rare butterfly (a stunt-double moth in the film) is bedeviled by an adolescent neighbor who stows away on his expedition. *The Blue Butterfly* is about a Canadian entomologist who takes a dying boy to South America to glimpse a blue morpho. And in *Jurassic Park*, skeptical scientist Ian Malcolm articulates a theory from Michael Crichton's original novel. "Physics handles badly…anything to do with turbulence," Malcolm declares in the book. "The new theory . . . is called chaos theory. The shorthand is the 'butterfly effect.' A butterfly flaps its wings in Peking, and weather in New York is different."

Butterflies have flapped their wings on many postage stamps over the years. Several thousand varieties have appeared internationally, while in the United States the common buckeye, Baltimore checkerspot, Oregon swallowtail, California dogface, falcate orangetip, monarch, tiger swallowtail, and

Butterfly exhibit
Screened and glass-enclosed butterfly exhibits offer an opportunity to view butterfly species from around the world. (See Appendix for a listing of exhibits.) At Butterfly World in Coconut Creek, Florida, rotting bananas attract owl butterflies, morphos, crackers, and other species to feeding dishes

Shaus' swallowtail have all displayed their colors beside various postal denominations. Elsewhere, butterflies have surfaced in *The Far Side* and other cartoons, as well as in ads for vodka, computers, the Internet, and other services—typically to exploit their eye-grabbing colors.

Butterflies also adorn clothing (T-shirts, sweatshirts, panties, hats), beverage glasses, calendars, patches, purses, jewelry, beach towels, bumper stickers, garden flags, souvenirs, and nearly everything else in today's culture. Butterflies, in short, are perceived as "cool." They are identified with religious symbolism, environmental causes, the arts, gardening, home decorating, personal attire, and tattoos.

Some people even eat them—usually the larvae (*Megathymus* giant-skippers). Exported in cans from Mexico, they are typically served fried or roasted. "The canned worms are best eaten hot," Ronald Taylor writes in *Butterflies in My Stomach*, noting that the "worms" have a "pleasant nutty flavor." But the majority of willing subjects who sampled french-fried butterflies with wings "found this product distasteful," and one asserted it tasted "like a pier smells."

There's a long-standing debate whether the "worm" at the bottom of a bottle of tequila is authentic and enhances the flavor (or a consumer's sexual prowess). In fact, experts say, only U.S.-bottled tequila from Mexico includes a "worm" (often a giant-skipper caterpillar, but just as likely a moth), debunking the myth that Aztec priests added live *gusano* larvae to containers of liquor to give their contents a "life spirit." Mexican distillers sometimes put a maguey-plant caterpillar (the carpenter moth *Comadia redtenbacheri*) in

mescal, a single-distilled liquor made from any of five varieties of agave plants, but not in tequila, which is double-distilled and made exclusively from blue agave. The tequila worm, it appears, is essentially a publicity gimmick.

Because live butterflies are considerably more attractive than limp larvae, well-wishers have embraced the practice of releasing butterflies at weddings—a custom since borrowed by grand openings, memorial services, cancer-support meetings, divorce celebrations, and prison releases. The liberation of these pricey butterflies (which can cost $95 or more a dozen, plus overnight shipping) alarms environmentalists, who fear the spread of disease or genetically risky interbreeding with local populations. NABA President Jeffrey Glassberg complains that these butterflies are "not so much released as dumped on the ground," since they are shipped "imprisoned in tiny envelopes and boxes" and therefore often unable to fly.

The sale of butterflies is regulated by the U.S. Department of Agriculture, and only nine species can be transported across state lines in their natural range. Enthusiasts who wish to experience the sheer bliss of being surrounded by butterflies not indigenous to their region can visit dozens of butterfly houses in North America and Europe, where exotic species are imported and raised under proper humidity and temperature-controlled conditions with approved flowers and hostplants. Among the more popular American conservatories are Butterfly World (Coconut Creek, Florida); Butterfly Rainforest (Gainesville, Florida); Cecil B. Day Butterfly Center at Callaway Gardens (Pine Mountain, Georgia); Magic Wings Butterfly House and

It is easy to coax a dying or exhausted butterfly onto your finger.

—Annie Dillard, *Pilgrim at Tinker Creek* (1975)

Insectarium (Durham, North Carolina); Butterfly Pavilion and Insect Center (Westminster, Colorado); Butterfly House (Chesterfield, Missouri); Magic Wings Francis R. Redmond Conservatory (South Deerfield, Massachusetts); Judy Istock Butterfly Haven, Chicago Academy of Sciences (Illinois); Mackinac Island Butterfly House (Michigan); Smithsonian Insect Zoo (Washington, D.C.); and the annual butterfly exhibition at the American Museum of Natural History (New York City). More information about butterfly houses can be found in the appendix of this book and on the Internet at www.butterflywebsite.com and www.butterflyexhibitions.org.

Most of the chrysalides and adult insects in these conservatories come from butterfly farms and ranches around the world. Butterfly ranching has proven successful in Papua New Guinea, where threatened and endangered species—especially the spectacular birdwings—are sold by villages to government-regulated facilities for export. In Costa Rica, butterfly farms attract ecotourists and export thousands of pupae every week.

Butterfly buffs who prefer to watch their lepidopterans out-of-doors typically plant their own butterfly gardens, and dozens of books offer botanical information about which plants attract particular species. Alternatively, butterfliers can visit local nurseries, parks, and arboretums, where flowering plants and hostplants attract both native and migratory species. Or they can join the North American Butterfly Association (www.naba.org), Xerces Society, or other environmental groups and partici-

pate in outings and seasonal butterfly census counts. A number of butterfly festivals are held annually in the United States, including the Pacific Grove (California) Butterfly Festival in October, when monarchs migrate to overwintering sites in the town's pine groves; the Mount Magazine (Arkansas) International Butterfly Festival in June; the Haynesville (Louisiana) Celebration of Butterflies in September; and the Rio Grande Prix of Butterflying at the NABA International Butterfly Park in Mission, Texas, in October.

Clearly, humans over the centuries have forged a fascinating relationship with butterflies. Once upon a time, men, women, and children snatched up silk or cheesecloth nets and set out to bag as many butterflies as they could, dropping them into jars of potassium cyanide, then mounting and labeling them. Scientists, of course, collected specimens to study, compare, and marvel at the details of their beauty and anatomy. But today, with museums around the world housing magnificent collections (butterflies collected in the 1700s "are still in good condition," says authority James Tilden) and field guides and other volumes richly illustrated with color plates and photographs, there's far less need to snag butterflies. As research scientist Paul Opler puts it: collected specimens should be useful, "not just stockpiled."

Butterflies not only provide millions of people with hours of aesthetic pleasure, they also "improve your physical, mental, and spiritual condition," insists Glassberg. He's absolutely right. Butterflies and humans ultimately make marvelous companions.

Tagged monarch
A monarch butterfly (*Danaus plexippus*) resting on a purple coneflower displays a University of Kansas–Lawrence tag on its forewing, used by biologists to help track migratory flight patterns.

Chapter 2

Physical Characteristics and Behavior

Structure and Size

"It is astonishing how few people notice butterflies," renowned author and lepidopterist Vladimir Nabokov once declared. But people who do notice butterflies—and they represent all ages, genders, and cultures—often do so with a zeal and delight that make up for the indifference of others. Field marks (color and pattern), behavior, and locality help observers match a name to a specific butterfly, but body structure (form and shape) and size provide the initial clues to a creature's identity.

The body of an adult butterfly, like that of other insects, has three principal divisions: head, thorax, and abdomen. A hard, protective covering of plates called sclerites made of a horny substance called chitin creates a supportive exoskeleton, with thin, flexible membranes between each division. All three parts of the body have external appendages and are covered with scales and hairs called setae.

On the butterfly's head are two large compound eyes, two club-tipped antennae (skippers have hooked or pointed tips), a tubular proboscis, and a pair of labial palpi that flank the proboscis. Each compound eye, in turn, comprises thousands of tiny visual units known as ommatidia. Although these beveled eyes are "incapable of focusing" on details, research biologist Philip DeVries explains in his indispensable *Butterflies of Costa Rica*, they are "very sensitive" to motion, light, and select colors. One or more pairs of small ocelli, or "simple" eyes, may be present as well.

Antennae assess chemical and physical aspects of the environment. Chemical receptors in pits on the knob atop each segmented antenna respond to scents, especially airborne pheromones (signature scents produced as an enticement to, or rejection of, prospective mates) from other butterflies. Antennae are also sensitive to vibrations and sounds, and DeVries notes that they function as "sensory organs for finding food, for mating, [and] for balance during flight."

The proboscis is an extensible cylindrical tube, similar to a drinking straw, formed after the butterfly emerges from the chrysalis by two interlocking halves that join along grooves "like the zippers on some plastic bags," authority James Scott explains in his excellent *Butterflies of North America*.

Blue tiger
The blue tiger butterfly (*Danaus limniace*), an Indian species related to the monarch, sips nectar from a milkweed blossom.

When not in use, the proboscis coils up like a watch spring on the underside of the head. When the butterfly lands on a food source, it extends the organ and inserts it into the flower, rotting fruit, tree sap, carrion, dung, urine, or damp sand; a vacuum created by the contracting muscles then forces fluids through the tube. As the butterfly moves to another food source, muscles within its head "lift the whole proboscis like a crane," Scott notes. According to some researchers, labial palpi on each side of the proboscis may be vestigial remnants of the mandibles of chewing insects such as beetles or locusts; DeVries hypothesizes that certain species use their palpi to clean their eyes, like windshield wipers, after feeding on fruit or dung, or perhaps to remove mites.

The thorax is subdivided into three fused segments covered with scales and setae, each segment equipped with a pair of slender jointed legs. Sensory organs called tarsi on the tips of the feet help the insect taste and make it possible for females of some species to identify suitable hostplants. Claws on the feet assist with walking and clinging to vegetation. Attached to the middle and rear thoracic segments is a pair of wings (forewings and hindwings), which are thin, platelike membranes covered with scales and fine hairs. The four wings are supported by tubes, typically referred to as veins, although they transport fluid only when the adult first emerges from the pupal case. The soft wings of a newly emerged butterfly expand as hemolymph is pumped through these veins; after the fluid is withdrawn, the wings stiffen and dry.

"One of the things that I find especially intriguing about butterfly wings is their size: they are much larger than is necessary for flight," lepidopterist Phil Schappert observes. The four wings are synchronized in flight, thereby acting together, explains butterfly ecologist Marc Minno, "but each can be adjusted to move forward, however, dip, and swerve." Narrower wings, such as those of the zebra longwing (*Heliconius charitonius*), permit "unusual aerial acrobatics, such as flying sideways, backward, and even upside down," authority Matthew Douglas reports.

The adult butterfly's third body division, the abdomen, is composed of ten smaller segments. Contained within are the digestive tract, energy-storage structure (called the fat body), and reproductive and excretory organs. The abdomen ends with the external genitalia.

The structure and shape of other stages of a butterfly's life—egg, caterpillar, and chrysalis—are addressed in the subchapter

Zebra longwing
An adult zebra longwing's (*Heliconius charitonius*) large compound eye, coiled proboscis, and labial palpi are visible in this close-up of its head. This brushfoot butterfly appears to have only four legs rather than six, but a reduced pair of brushlike forelegs can be seen near the eye.

Metamorphosis, but it is interesting to note that while adult butterfly size remains constant upon emergence from the chrysalis, the caterpillar increases its size dramatically. To do so, the caterpillar must periodically shed its exoskeleton, splitting the hardened or chitonized head and the dead outer layer of abdominal skin anywhere from four to nine times. "Essentially, their skin is like a trash bag," says Florida entomologist Jaret Daniels. "It is packed full of food until there is no more room. Once full, it is discarded for a larger, baggier one underneath." As they increase their size from molt to molt, caterpillars grow "almost exponentially," Schappert notes, which explains their reputation as "eating machines." By the time they form a chrysalis, he adds, caterpillars can be three thousand to four thousand times larger in volume and mass than at the time of their hatching.

The "size" of a particular butterfly species is determined not by its average weight (most butterflies weigh less than a paper clip, Douglas points out) or by measuring its body length but usually by reporting the range of adult wingspans or the length of the forewing. Ranges are useful for describing wingspans because adult males and females that are conspecific (i.e., of the same species) can differ dramatically in size, and butterflies that develop during different seasons or weather conditions can vary as well.

With such variations among butterflies, it's no wonder some dispute remains regarding the world's "largest" and "smallest" species. Still, most experts agree that the female Queen Alexandra's birdwing (*Ornithoptera alexandrae*) from Papua New Guinea holds the record for the world's largest butterfly with a wingspan of up to 11 inches (28 cm). The claim to the title of the world's smallest butterfly belongs either to the Western pygmy blue (*Brephidium exilis*) of North America, whose wingspan ranges from ⅜ to ¾ inch (10 to 19 mm); the dwarf blue (*B. barberae*) of South Africa, with a wingspan of about ½ inch (12 mm); or the Sinai baton blue (*Pseudophilotes sinaicus*) of Egypt, with a minimum forewing length of about ¼ inch (6.25 mm).

Scales and Coloration

The great French entomologist J. Henri Fabre once called butterflies "the aristocracy not of instinct but of dress." Indeed, the splendor of their dress is what sets butterflies apart from other insects. That's because the wings of butterflies are covered with thousands of scales, overlapping like tiles on a roof, and each scale has its own pigment or produces color by diffraction. These two systems—pigmentary and structural coloration—create the tapestry of hues we associate with butterflies, and, scale by scale, they are primarily responsible for the individuality of each species.

The scales on butterfly wings and bodies are typically characterized as modified "hairs," but, more accurately, they are multicellular protuberances called setae, which, in the case of butterflies, display a single pigment each or are covered with light-refracting ridges and grooves. A single butterfly typically has only four or five different pigments, but because the scales are so tiny, explains Douglas, "thousands of differently colored scales may

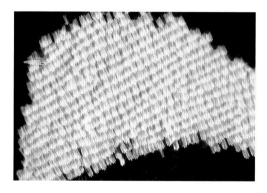

Eastern tiger swallowtail setae
Rows of tiny scales, or setae, visible in this extreme close-up of a yellow spot on the wing of an Eastern tiger swallowtail (*Pterourus glaucus*), overlap like shingles on a roof.

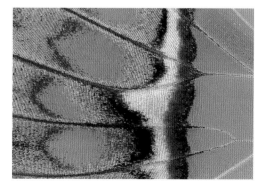

Malachite wing
Wing detail of a malachite butterfly (*Siproeta stelenes*).

Female great Mormon

Sexual dimorphism—i.e., variation in form and color between males and females of the same species—is pronounced in the great Mormon butterfly (*Papilio memnon*) of Indo-Australia. The forewings of the female are generally pale brown and the hindwings dark, with red warning colors and prominent tails.

I spotted the monarch as it rose: a russet vision like a fox darting from its green covert.

—Robert Michael Pyle, *Chasing Monarchs: Migrating with the Butterflies of Passage* (1999)

be optically blended by our brains to produce a myriad of different hues and intensities." The critical pigments are melanins—which are responsible for blacks, grays, browns, tans, rusts, and some reds and yellows—and pterins—which generate radiant reds, oranges, yellows, and some white.

The iridescent blues, violets, greens, and coppers seen in some butterflies are generated by refraction, or bending, of light waves. Called "interference colors," these iridescent tones are "very pure and brilliant," naturalist Hilda Simon reports; they undergo "a rainbowlike play and change of hues" and appear only when wavelengths "neutralize and eliminate one another, so that only one color of the spectrum is reflected. With every change of the light angle, a different color appears."

The colors and patterns produced by these scales perform several functions, among them promoting species and mate identification. Drab or cryptic colors camouflage an insect from predators, while bright colors as a rule communicate a warning that a butterfly is unpalatable or dangerously toxic. "It would seem suicidal for a butterfly group to be colored like neon signs, seeming to say 'eat me,'" observes naturalist John Kricher, but "obviousness" can provide a critical warning. Scales also improve aerodynamic efficiency by contributing to lift.

Intense colors and ornate markings such as eyespots may startle or intimidate predators, and mimicry of similar-looking but risk-laden species offers protection by association. Body and wing scales provide

other benefits as well: they help to insulate the insect during cold weather, and dark pigments warm the body by absorbing radiant heat from the sun, just as lighter colored pigments absorb less heat where temperatures are already warm.

The amount of pigment, usually melanin, associated with a particular species can vary according to season, altitude, and latitude. Males sometimes differ in color or pattern from females of the same species—a phenomenon called sexual dimorphism—while individuals of some species look completely different from other members of the same sex. Some female Eastern tiger swallowtails (*Pterourus glaucus*) in the eastern and southern United States, for example, have a black rather than a yellow ground color, mimicking the chemically distasteful pipevine swallowtail (*Battus philenor*). Color variations may exist among regional populations of a single species as well, as in the case of clippers (*Parthenos sylvia*) across Asia and races of the postman (*Heliconius melpomene*) and small postman (*H. erato*) in Central and South America.

Other morphs, or variants, occur as well, including genetic mutants called gynandromorphs whose wings may be "male" on one side of the body but "female" on the opposite side. And some butterfly species and subfamilies—e.g., the glasswings (*Cithaerias*) of Central America—have transparent forewings that render them relatively invisible when flying low over the forest floor or resting on the underside of a leaf.

Wings, Flight, and Locomotion

When Wilbur and Orville Wright were pondering ways to build a manned flying machine, they spent hours observing nature. Above all, they studied birds and butterflies to understand how to achieve a balance among the forces of lift, drift, and gravity. Later, they shared their discovery with the editor of *Gleanings in Bee Culture*: "When some large bird or butterfly is soaring with motionless wings, a very little power from behind will keep it moving. Well, if this motion is kept up, a very little incline of the wings will keep it from falling. A little more incline, and a little more push from behind, and the bird or the butterfly, or the machine created by human hands, will gradually rise in the air."

It was a critical discovery and, with the help of propellers, advanced their dream of machine-powered flight. Of course, birds and butterflies worked this out millions of years earlier, yet even today the miracle of their flight excites observers.

Athis
Wings of butterfly species vary significantly in size and shape. Members of the genus *Heliconius*, which includes this pair of athis butterflies (*H. athis*) from Ecuador, are commonly called longwings because of their distinctively elongated wings.

A butterfly's wings, rather than its legs, provide the principal means of locomotion. Wings come in many shapes and sizes, but there are always four, and they consist of two sheets of cuticular membrane covered with scales and supported by a structural framework of veins—like struts or joists in a house frame. By alternately contracting and relaxing muscles in its thorax, a butterfly is able to flap its wings, generating flight "when the upward force or lift exceeds the downward-pulling force of gravity," Douglas explains. "For an average-size butterfly, the flight muscles are very strong relative to the weight of the body. The forward motion provided by the angled upstroke and downstroke of the wings creates thrust, but wind exerts a force termed drag on any object." Which is why, he points out, butterflies are seldom seen flying on extremely windy days.

The flight of butterflies can assume a variety of styles, depending on the individual, species, environmental conditions, and other variables. Many butterflies employ a fluttering or slow-hovering "flap and glide" technique, relying on the downward power strokes of their wings to produce lift, then "parachute-gliding" by creating a concave undersurface with their wings. The result is a "rather lazy flapping flight," Rod and Ken Preston-Mafham observe. Another style of flight, called whirring, is so fast that observers see only a blur; it is commonly used by skippers and during mating maneuvers by male *Papilio* swallowtails and male *Pieris* whites. While the wings beat at a rate of about five to ten times per second during normal flapping, the wingbeat in whirring flight can be twenty-five to

one hundred beats per second, according to Walter Linsenmaier. The fastest butterflies have been clocked, in brief spurts, at speeds of up to 50 miles per hour (80 km/h).

Other recognizable flight styles include swooping—employed by morphos, which have unusually large wings—and spiraling, used by European speckled wood butterflies (*Pararge aegeria*) and others during territorial skirmishes. The unusual flight behavior of the postman and several other Neotropical heliconids was described in 1901 by observer David Sharp as "concerted dances, rising and falling in the air like gnats; when some of them withdraw from the concert, others fill their places."

Butterfly watchers can attest to the fact that different species vary in the heights they fly. Scott estimates that most fly about one-half to one meter (roughly 2 to 3 feet) above

Golden birdwing
The wings of a golden birdwing butterfly (*Troides rhadamantus*) in flight, photographed at a very slow shutter speed, appear blurred to show the motion.

Man with all his looms and dyes cannot create anything half so exquisite as a butterfly's wing.

—Donald Culross Peattie

Zebra swallowtail wing
Detail of the underside of a zebra swallowtail (*Eurytides marcellus*) highlights the zebra-striped pattern of scales on the wing membrane and the supporting framework of veins.

protection by mimicking the familiar foliage or leaf litter of the habitat.

Wings also play a role in a butterfly's thermoregulation: lighter colors reflect the heat of the sun, while darker colors absorb rays and warm the insect during basking. Also, according to Douglas, the fanning of wings by some species may prevent overheating by cooling the air over the thorax.

The wings of certain species send signals of a defensive nature: eyespots, for example, may intimidate predators by mimicking the eyes of birds of prey, snakes, frogs, or lizards. Eyespots also may lure the jaws of predators away from the butterfly's body and head, as do the "tails" on swallowtails, ruddy daggerwings (*Marpesia petreus*), common clubtails (*Parides coon*), and common imperials (*Cheritra freja*). Large eyespots, such as those on owl butterflies (*Caligo*), buckeyes (*Junonia coenia*), and peacocks (*Inachis io*), may also startle intruders, providing a few crucial seconds to escape. Wing markings can be aposematic: brightly colored—often yellow or red—to attract the attention of a predator (i.e., one with a memory of a previous encounter) and at the same time warn of toxicity or unpalatability.

As a territorial defense, wings can make a threatening motion or other conspicuous movement to alert a rival or an intruder to the wing-flapper's presence. And, of course, the colors and patterns advertise the butterfly's species and its gender to other butterflies.

While wings offer the principal means of locomotion, an adult butterfly also has three pairs of legs, each comprising five main sections and attached to the thorax for perching. (Among nymphalid, or brushfoot,

the ground, although some blues fly only a few centimeters above ground, swallowtails often fly several meters high, and some hairstreaks keep to the canopy of trees. Migrant butterflies can be seen considerably higher, and swarms of monarchs have been tracked by radar at up to 5,000 feet (1,524 m) above ground.

Wings, of course, do more than provide convenient transportation. They also provide camouflage, assist in thermoregulation, and display defensive, territorial, and sexual signals. The cryptic wing colors and patterns of many butterflies—often noticeable on the underside of the wings, which are held upright by many species when at rest—have evolved to enhance survival from predators. In some cases (e.g., the leaf butterflies of Asia and the raggedy-looking anglewings of North America), the shape of the wing in conjunction with the butterfly's resting position provides

butterflies, the two forelegs have degenerated to stubs modified for tasting.) Caterpillars have legs, too—ten prolegs in pairs on certain abdominal segments and six thoracic legs that correspond to the adult legs. When caterpillars walk, they sway their head and lay down a silk thread that DeVries dubs a "safety line," since it helps to prevent the larva from falling off a hostplant and starving.

Internal Anatomy

While the razzle-dazzle of a butterfly's external finery can be astonishing, its internal anatomy is far more conventional. In fact, a butterfly has fundamentally the same internal organ systems as other insects and animals—with several significant differences.

Unlike mammals, butterflies do not have a network of veins and arteries (or blood, in the traditional sense). Instead, the circulatory system of a butterfly is an "open" system that bathes the body's organs and tissues in emerald-green hemolymph, pumped by the expansion and contraction of the abdomen. "Cut an insect and it bleeds, more often than not to death," observe Rod and Ken Preston-Mafham. The butterfly's heart is a tubelike vessel that runs the full length of the abdomen and loops in the thorax. It pumps hemolymph forward to the head during contraction and back into the thorax during expansion. Unlike blood, hemolymph has no hemoglobin; instead, its main component is water, which acts as a solvent for various molecules. The circulatory system also delivers nutrients and carries away waste products.

In humans and other vertebrates, oxygen is transported through blood vessels from the lungs to other parts of the body via the hemoglobin in red blood cells, but a butterfly has no lungs. Instead, oxygen enters the thorax and abdomen through holes called spiracles and is carried directly to body tissues via tiny air tubes called tracheae. The tracheae, in turn, branch into minute tracheoles, where the actual gas exchange takes place. The butterfly's body movements coordinate with the opening and closing of spiracles, permitting air to be drawn in through some spiracles and out others. When oxygen is not needed, the spiracles close to minimize water loss. Most flying insects also have air sacs that collapse and expand like bellows to bolster the passage of air through the tracheal system, authority Jon Harrison explains.

The digestive system of an adult butterfly accommodates its feeding method (sucking with a proboscis) and its diet of flower nectar and liquids from other sources, including rotting fruit, bird droppings, dung, urine, and pollen mixed with nectar. Utilizing powerful muscles, the pharynx pumps food into an enlargement of the closed digestive tract called the crop, where the food is stored. Digestion and absorption of nutrients then take place in the middle portion of the tract, called the midgut. Some absorbed food is converted into fat and stored in a reserve called the fat body, for use by hibernating species and females during reproduction. When a large quantity of liquid food has been ingested, the abdomen stretches to accommodate it—something DeVries has noted occurring among morphos, owl

I dreamt I was a butterfly, fluttering hither and dither, to all intents and purposes a butterfly. I was conscious only of following my fancies as a butterfly, and was unconscious of my individuality as a man. Suddenly I awoke and there I lay myself again. Now I do not know whether I was then a man dreaming I was a butterfly or whether I am now a butterfly dreaming I am a man.

—Chuang-tsu, fourth century B.C.

butterflies, and mothlike *Brassolis* butterflies that feed on rotting fruit. Since insects lack kidneys, they produce a solid product called uric acid, which is encased in a thin membrane and transported to the rear of the midgut by the Malpighian tubules. Waste products are then forced into the hindgut, where the muscular rectum stores feces until voiding them through the anus.

Besides the digestive system, the abdomen houses the reproductive tract and, at the end, the genitalia. In females, the final segments of the abdomen contain the ovaries, oviduct, sperm-storage sac, and ovipositor; in males, the testes, sperm-storage sac, seminal vesicles, aedeagus (phallus), and exterior claspers. Scientists have discovered that dissection of male and female genitals is extremely useful in identifying certain species. The butterfly's central nervous system resembles that of other insects. A ventral nerve cord runs beneath the alimentary canal, and knots of nerve cells called ganglia appear at intervals and direct activities of body parts surrounding them. The most prominent ganglion, the brain, is situated in the head.

Vision

The eyes of a butterfly, British entomologist E. B. Ford once declared, "differ from our own eyes in almost every possible respect." Indeed, the highly intricate compound eye of a butterfly comprises as many as 17,000 photoreceptive elements called ommatidia, each capped with a hexagonal lens, or facet, that gathers light. (The human eye, on the other hand, has a single lens.) Each facet trans-

mits "a portion of the total picture," notes zoologist Thomas Emmel, with the result "comparable to the pixels or dots that make up a picture on a computer screen." The final image is "a single, integrated scene," Pyle explains, but its resolution is poor, estimated to be only about I percent as sharp as a human's.

While sacrificing acuity, the butterfly eye is a superior instrument for detecting movement, enjoying a much broader field of vision (well over 300 degrees) than the human eye's 200-degree field. The structure of the compound eye permits a butterfly to see in all directions, lepidopterist Jo Brewer says, "except directly beneath its body."

Perhaps even more remarkable is the eye's spectral range, which authority Robert Silberglied calls "the broadest visible spectrum known in the animal kingdom." Butterflies can discriminate all colors visible to humans and ultraviolet, too, which is valuable for detecting hostplants and flowers and choosing a mate.

Heliconids, or longwings, are believed to be "the most highly developed in the butterfly world," author Patrick Hook says, and the small postman in particular exhibits enhanced vision in the yellow portion of the spectrum, probably due to its preference for yellow flowers. In midmorning, however, "something in the brain switches their sight to being predominantly in the red part of the spectrum," Hook notes. "This is because the females have distinctive red markings on their wings, which the males use as signals for courtship to begin. They will then inspect anything that is red." Collectors of blue

Male and female postman
A male postman butterfly (*Heliconius melpomene*) hovers over a female, which he identifies by color and other features. Butterflies can discriminate all colors of the spectrum visible to humans, as well as the near ultraviolet range, and heliconian vision is among the most highly developed of all butterflies.

Monarch
Close-up of the head of a monarch butterfly (*Danaus plexippus*). The large compound eyes comprise thousands of photoreceptive elements, capped with lenses called facets, which transmit an integrated image like a computer graphic consisting of thousands of pixels.

Eastern tiger swallowtail caterpillar
Eyespots, or false eyes, on the head of an Eastern tiger swallowtail caterpillar *(Pterourus [Papilio] glaucus)* and on other swallowtail larvae resemble snake eyes and offer protection from predators. The caterpillar's real eyes are the tiny dots on the side of its face.

morphos exploit the male butterfly's similar curiosity by waving scraps of blue silk on poles in order to lure precious specimens closer to the ground.

The compound eyes of skippers apparently can better focus light on the retina than can the eyes of other butterflies, which permits them to fly faster with greater accuracy. Butterfly caterpillars have eyes, too, but their eyes are considerably smaller than those of adults and consist of only six ommatidia. Caterpillar eyes possess an adult's sensitivity to color and ultraviolet light, but, according to Emmel, most larvae are unable to see beyond a few inches.

Smell and Taste

Residents of the eastern and southern United States and other parts of the world are sometimes startled to see a butterfly sporting an inordinately long, Cyrano de Bergerac-esque "snout"—one that would appear to give snout butterflies (*Libytheana*) an advantage in the smelling department. But this beaklike snout is actually a pair of prodigious palpi; butterflies, it turns out, have no nose.

That doesn't mean they have no sense of smell, however; they utilize nerve cells exposed to the surface through olfactory pits in the exoskeleton or on setae. These hairlike bristles act as sensory receptors that assess the chemical and physical properties of the environment; "those detecting airborne chemicals account for smell, while those that perceive chemicals through direct contact with solids or liquids allow an insect

to taste," entomologist Rick Imes explains. (Tactile setae are found on virtually all parts of the adult body, including special scales on the wings, as well as on a caterpillar's body.)

The olfactory sense in most insects is "keener than anything we can imagine," says Imes; in butterflies, the prime location for smell is the antennae, where the clubs at the tip harbor most of the sense organs. Researchers have discovered that olfactory pegs on the antennae of females can detect male pheromones, food, water, and suitable plants on which to deposit eggs. (In addition to smell and taste, receptors on the antennae perform functions related to touch and hearing.) Organs of taste are also present on the adult's proboscis, palpi, and legs, as well as on the mouth and mouthparts of the caterpillar.

Taste receptors on the legs respond to dissolved sugars and induce sipping of flower nectar via the proboscis. In their maternal quest for suitable plants on which to lay eggs, some females "drum" on prospective host-plants with their forelegs, puncturing the plants with spines on the lower surface of their legs to release juices and odors. These, in turn, are sampled and assessed by the taste receptors.

Adult *Heliconius* butterflies—and perhaps others—have tiny comblike olfactory hairs on the tip of their proboscis, Scott reports, which they use to collect bundles of pollen. When fluid is discharged from the proboscis onto the pollen, nutrients in the pollen are dissolved and can be sucked up through the proboscis.

Black and white heliconian
Feeding on pollen permits heliconid butterflies such as this black and white heliconian (*Heliconius cydno*) to live longer than most other species. After collecting highly nutritious granules on its proboscis, the butterfly pumps up fluid to melt the pollen, then digests the rich liquid.

Food Sources and Hostplants

DeVries, whose authoritative *Butterflies of Costa Rica* is highly useful even for enthusiasts unlikely to ever set foot in a rain forest, studied botany in college when his friends were studying butterflies. DeVries "couldn't compete" in the field, writes Russell, "so he changed the rules: He found what the caterpillars were eating." Indeed, finding the hostplants and nectar plants, rather than chasing the butterflies themselves, can pay off handsomely for amateurs and professionals alike.

That's because caterpillars and adults, as a rule, are "diet specific": larvae commonly feed on plants of a single family, and adults seek nectar from flowers—or fluids from sap, pollen, rotting fruit and vegetables, carrion, bird droppings, urine, or dung. Since adults cannot chew solid foods, they obtain most of their energy-rich carbohydrates and nitrogen-rich amino acids from the sugary nectars or other fluids they sip. "Butterflies apparently have a 'sweet tooth,'" says author Norman Riley; "they can detect sugar in a mixture of one part to 300,000, whereas we poor humans can detect sweetness only where there is at least one part sugar in 200."

Adults are less choosy than larvae about their food, and their quest for nectar can take them to "dozens or hundreds of kinds

Red admiral
A red admiral (*Vanessa atalanta*) extends its flexible strawlike proboscis into rotting fruit to suck up fluids. Many butterflies are attracted to rotting fruit, tree sap, dung, urine, carrion, and other strong-smelling food sources that the average person does not associate with these delicate creatures.

of flowers," Scott reports. Butterfly bushes, milkweed, lantana, lavender, hibiscus, lilac, pentas, phlox, zinnia, marigold, clover, and thistle are among the more popular flowering plants visited by adult butterflies in the United States. While making their rounds, butterflies unwittingly pick up tiny pollen sacs and transport them to other flowers, facilitating cross-pollination. While some butterflies are attracted to one color or another (sulphurs and swallowtails seem to like red flowers, for example), most show little color preference at all. Butterflies are able to see the entire color spectrum ("the widest visual spectrum of any animal," says Schappert), including ultraviolet, which creates attractive ring patterns, or nectar guides, in certain flowers.

But forest butterflies—which encounter few flowers in the understory of dense trees—and certain other species, such as hackberry butterflies (*Asterocampa celtis*), rarely visit flowers, and others never feed at all during their brief adult lives. *Heliconius* females are unusual because they feed on pollen, and their foraging has been compared to trap-lining by humans: each female repeatedly visits a string of flowers in the same sequence, Douglas says, "minimizing energy expenditure." Species that prefer alternative foods, such as overripe fruit and vegetables, can be easily lured to bait set out by collectors, and field researchers cheerfully confess to emptying their bladders in the name of science to produce pungent pools of urine popular for their sodium content. Animal dung has its fans, too, and the Preston-Mafhams claim that leopard droppings are particularly irresistible. In Kenya, they once spied a "living quilt" of *Charaxes*

butterflies on a "juicy morsel" of leopard dung; the butterflies were so absorbed in pushing and shoving that many permitted themselves to be gently stroked.

Male butterflies crave salts, probably to replace the sodium they surrender in spermatophores passed along to females during copulation. The result is a curious phenomenon called "mud-puddling." Dozens, hundreds, or thousands of butterflies will congregate in "puddle clubs" on damp ground or along sandy or muddy riverbanks, where they extract salts dissolved in the mineral-laden water. Sometimes these butterflies squirt droplets from their anus or discharge liquid from their proboscis while imbibing the salty moisture. Butterflies are also renowned for their love of salty human perspiration, and some julias have been seen sipping liquid from the corner of a crocodilian's eye in Brazil and the eyes of turtles in Peru.

Caterpillars are widely associated with diet specificity—in this case, hostplants whose leaves, stems, or flowers attract a particular species. Milkweeds, for example, are linked to monarchs, whose larvae have evolved a tolerance for the plants' poisons; they can ingest the toxic chemicals and store them in their bodies, providing a defense against predators not only in the larval stage but also the adult form.

Similarly, toxic passionflower vines are hostplants to Gulf fritillaries and other heliconians, triggering what scientists have called an escalating "arms race" between the plants and the insects. Since the larvae have evolved an immunity to the toxic chemicals, many passionflower vines (of which there are some five hundred known species) have evolved an

I confess I do not believe in time. I like to fold my magic carpet, after use, in such a way as to superimpose one part of the pattern upon another. Let visitors trip. And the highest enjoyment of timelessness—in a landscape selected at random—is when I stand among rare butterflies and their food plants. This is ecstasy, and behind the ecstasy is something else, which is hard to explain. It is like a momentary vacuum into which rushes all that I love.

—Vladimir Nabokov, *Speak, Memory: An Autobiography Revisited* (1966)

Mud-puddling butterflies
Rain forest butterflies congregate in swarms in Peru's Amazon River Basin, demonstrating a common behavior called "mud-puddling." The butterflies, primarily males, extract salts from the damp ground that are essential for successful breeding.

Julia
This tropical Julia butterfly *(Dryas iulia)*, like a number of other species, obtains basic nutrients by sipping liquids from bird droppings through its proboscis.

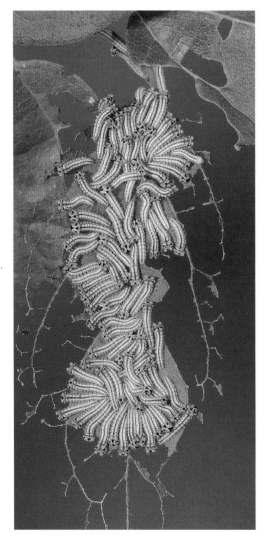

Tawny emperor caterpillars
Tawny emperor caterpillars *(Asterocampa clyton)* feed communally, rather than individually, on hackberry leaves. A mass of larvae will skeletonize the leaves of a hostplant like miniature eating machines.

array of other defenses: some have altered the shape of their leaves, for example, to deceive the butterflies, while others have developed tougher, thicker leaves. One tropical passionflower has evolved hooked spines that ensnare the larvae, then disembowel them or hold them until they die. Others generate false stipules—projections from the leaf stem—that look inviting to egg-laying females. After the eggs are laid, the bogus stipules drop off and carry the eggs to their doom.

Not all larvae consume plants, however. Harvester caterpillars are carnivorous, Paul Opler notes, feeding on woolly aphids and sometimes on ant brood in their nests, and according to entomologists Valerio Sbordoni and Saverio Forestiero, the larvae of green hairstreaks *(Callophrys rubi)* and several species of blues are occasionally cannibalistic.

Communication

Communication, typically defined as the exchange of information, occurs primarily, though not exclusively, among members of the same species. Insects communicate via all five animal senses (vision, smell, taste, touch, and hearing), but other "unknown methods" may be used as well, says Rick Imes.

Vision, or photoreception, is the principal means by which butterflies sense, identify, and locate members of their own species, prospective mates, rivals, predators, prey, and other objects or phenomena. Because their eyes are unusually sensitive to light and color, butterflies transmit visual signals to one another via distinctive wing colors and patterns. These cues, in turn, assist in species recognition for reproduction or for aggregation behaviors such as roosting, migration, or overwintering. Other visual signals and responses are critical in courtship rituals such as zigzag dances, wing waves, rejection dances, and bowing, and for judging the size and fitness of partners.

Sexual communication in butterflies is not exclusively visual, however. Chemoreception of pheromones and other substances involves smell and taste. Chemosensory setae—located on the body but concentrated on the antennae, legs, and mouthparts—detect airborne chemicals for olfactory sampling of the environment, while other molecules absorbed through pathways in cuticular pores are processed for taste.

Touch in insects is detected by tactile setae found on most parts of the adult (antennae, wings, legs, proboscis, head, thorax, and abdomen) and nearly everywhere on the larva, Scott explains; setae are connected to nerve cells beneath the exoskeleton that send signals to the brain. Touch can identify movement, substrate vibrations, and the presence of objects and chemicals, and it is sometimes a behavioral component during antenna or wing contact in courtship and territorial defense.

A more recently investigated mode of communication involves hearing and transmission of acoustic signals to conspecifics, intruders, and predators. In Central and South America, *Hamadryas* butterflies (variable crackers and others) make loud wing clicks during chases and other interactions with conspecific rivals. Since many scientists once thought butterflies could not hear, this finding seemed incompatible—until researchers determined that *Hamadryas* and several other species have a thin translucent tympanal membrane called Vogel's organ at the base of the forewing, stretched across two large air sacs, which responds to sound. Patches of hair (chaetosemata) located at the back of the head in adults were also found to detect sound, touch, and air vibrations.

Further evidence of hearing turned up in primitive nocturnal mothlike butterflies of the superfamily Hedyloidea, which, according to entomologist Jayne Yack, had an "ultrasonic ear"—perhaps a degenerate "bat detector." In 2004, researchers Mirian Hay-Roe and

Large tree nymphs
During the courtship ritual of the large tree nymph, or paper kite (*Idea leuconoe*), the male communicates sexually by hovering over the female and wafting pheromones from his extended hair pencils— the bright yellow brushes hanging from the tip of his abdomen.

Blue-and-white longwing
Field-collected blue-and-white longwings (*Heliconius cydno*) from Ecuador have produced wing-click sounds in a greenhouse when encountering butterflies of their own and other species, suggesting previously unknown acoustic communication among longwings.

Richard Mankin reported that field-collected blue-and-white longwings (*Heliconius cydno alithea*) from Ecuador, when introduced to a greenhouse insectary in Texas, produced previously unreported sounds during encounters with conspecifics during the day and at roosting time, as well as during aggressive encounters with female *Heliconius erato* (the small postman). For unknown reasons, the *Heliconius* stopped producing audible sounds after one month, and the next generation raised in the greenhouse failed to produce sounds altogether. Nonetheless, the authors write, evidence of these sounds suggests that "wing clicks may play a role in both intra- and interspecific communication among *Heliconius* species."

Some caterpillars are reported to produce acoustic signals when engaged in symbiotic relationships with ants—and ants signal back. Caterpillar and ant calls are not identical, DeVries observes, but they are similar ("no mean feat for a caterpillar!"). These low-amplitude signals are transmitted through foodplants or other surfaces, and the ants detect the vibrations with their feet.

Survival Mechanisms

"Butterflies are free," Charles Dickens declared in *Bleak House*, but to stay that way, and remain one flap ahead of their enemies, butterflies require a full repertoire of defenses. These defenses fall into essentially four categories—appearance, physical armaments, behavior, and chemical defenses—and typically work in concert, DeVries says.

The outward appearance of an adult butterfly, chrysalis, caterpillar, or egg offers several lines of defense, but foremost is the actual resemblance to its surroundings. Many adults depend on cryptic coloration to deceive predators by blending with their background. The undersides of wings, which are customarily exposed when a butterfly is at rest, are often a mix of drab earth tones—brown, tan, gray, and black—to conceal the insect on leaves, bark, twigs, or soil. Chrysalides, too, are often dull gray or brown and resemble a dead leaf. Many caterpillars, on the other hand, are green, which provides camouflage on hostplant leaves and stems, while butterfly eggs are frequently yellow green or white.

Disruptive coloration, another survival mechanism, encompasses patterns, stripes, patches, and other often bright designs to interrupt the otherwise familiar outline of a butterfly's wings. Among tropical clearwing butterflies, the absence of wing scales altogether allows species to hide in plain sight, their transparent wings blending into the background. Another effective defense is aposematic coloration—dramatic hues that boldly advertise distastefulness to predators sensitized by previous disagreeable encounters.

Mimicry counts among the best-known defense mechanisms, and all forms of butterflies, not just adults, are accomplished impersonators. Leaves, rocks, sticks, snakes, even bird droppings are mimicked. But, in one of nature's most dramatic performances, some adults masquerade as other species, acting almost as if their lives depended on it. And, it turns out, they often do.

Butterfly mimicry among unrelated species was first described by Henry Walter Bates, an enthusiastic English naturalist who collected specimens in the Amazon from 1848 to 1859 and published an account of his travels and research in 1863. Astonished by the profusion of insects he encountered during his 1,400-mile journey up the Amazon, Bates collected some 14,000 distinct species. Their sheer numbers, he wrote, were due to an abundance of food, warm temperatures, absence of extremely cold seasons, and other factors—but what he found particularly striking were the similarities of wing colors and patterns among unrelated species of butterflies inhabiting the same habitat. From his observations, he developed the first theory of mimicry, later called Batesian mimicry in his honor.

The butterfly model, Bates recognized, was invariably an unpalatable or noxious species whose mimic was an edible one. During the course of natural selection, a mimic—

Question mark
A mottled light-brown underside and jagged leaflike wings provide camouflage for the question mark butterfly (*Polygonia interrogationis*) when it lands on dead leaves or tree bark.

despite its palatability—would enjoy protection in that locality from predators that confused the mimic's colors or patterns with those of the model. "A bird that eats a toxic butterfly becomes violently ill," Brewer explains; "it does not die but soon recovers. The toxic butterfly attacked or eaten does die, but the whole species or whole colony gains protection by the sacrifice of a single individual because, having recovered, the bird thereafter associates the colors and/or pattern of the toxic butterfly with its bad effects and avoids similar colors and patterns in choosing its prey."

In North America, the most cited Batesian mimic is the viceroy (*Limenitis archippus*), whose bright orange-and-black wings mimic those of the bad-tasting monarch, queen (*Danaus gilippus*), and soldier

Question mark chrysalis
The shape and cryptic coloration of a question mark butterfly's chrysalis offer protection by mimicking dead leaves dangling from a stem.

Snout caterpillar
The green caterpillar of a snout butterfly (*Libytheana carinenta*) closely matches the color and texture of the hackberry leaves on which it feeds.

Giant swallowtail caterpillar
The caterpillar of a giant swallowtail (*Heraclides [Papilio] cresphontes*), whose shiny skin and cryptic coloration are easily mistaken for fresh bird droppings, everts red forked osmeteria as a defense mechanism when threatened. A drop of strong-smelling fluid is visible on the tip of one of the extended horns.

Spicebush swallowtail caterpillar
A spicebush swallowtail caterpillar (*Pterourus [Papilio] troilus*) hides in a rolled-up leaf shelter by day to protect itself and displays a pair of giant eyespots on the thorax, mimicking the head and eyes of a snake.

(*D. eresimus*) butterflies. Researchers have recently determined that the viceroy itself is distasteful, storing bitter-tasting but less toxic salicylic acid (aspirin) compounds from its willow hostplant while feeding as a caterpillar. One familiar example of Batesian mimicry that pushes the limits of the ratio of good-tasting mimics to bad-tasting models is the one in which several common North American swallowtails—the black swallowtail (*Papilio polyxenes*), the spicebush swallowtail (*P. troilus*), the palamedes swallowtail (*Pterourus palamedes*), and a regional color morph of the female Eastern tiger swallowtail—all mimic the highly distasteful pipevine swallowtail (*Battus philenor*). Neotropical examples from this complex include *Dismorphia* butterflies and their nasty-tasting *Heliconius* and *Mechanitis* counterparts.

To explain how unpalatable species might benefit from a mutual resemblance, German naturalist Fritz Müller demonstrated in 1879 that when two or more distasteful species look alike, a predator requires only one disastrous encounter, not two, to become sensitized. "All the bad-tasting mimics gain," explains Russell, "as they reinforce the predator's understanding not to eat any of them. Fewer of any one species get tested. Everyone wins." Müllerian mimicry occurs in a number of noxious white butterflies of the genus *Pieris* (the cabbage white, mustard white, and others), whose larvae ingest oils and glycosides from mustard hostplants; and more than a dozen regional color variations of the small postman, or erato (*Heliconius erato*), and the postman (*H. melpomene*) in Central and South America.

Other mimicry convergence among groups of butterflies is exhibited in "mimicry rings" that comprise Müllerian mimics (and some day-flying moths) *and* Batesian mimics. These rings are identified by distinct color complexes (tiger, red, blue, orange, and transparent), embracing dozens of nearly indistinguishable species and making their identification, in Kricher's words, "a taxonomist's nightmare."

If nature's art is the first line of defense for many butterflies, a second line is protective armament. Some African *Charaxes* have a row of miniscule "teeth" on the leading edge of their forewings, possibly to deter birds, as do some Neotropical swallowtails. More important, many caterpillars are equipped with weapons—irritant spines and hairs; clubs on the thorax to deflect ants; and tentacles that pop out from the abdomen—while the chrysalides of some skippers sport a long, threatening horn on the head.

Behavioral defenses include the ready options of flight (to escape earthbound predators) and hiding in nearby trees, shrubs, grasses, rocky areas, or other sanctuaries. Overwintering adults may take advantage of cracks or holes in trees, and some caterpillars stitch or roll up leaves with silk and conceal themselves within. Other caterpillars create "frass chains," repositioning their solid excrement to deceive predatory ants. Caterpillars of the silver-spotted skipper (*Epargyreus clarus*) can even eject their fecal pellets more than a meter from their leaf shelters to confuse nearby predators. Some caterpillars, when startled or harassed, simply drop off a plant like a bungee jumper, hanging suspended by a thread, or go limp and fall. And the gregarious caterpillars of some species respond in concert, twitching and jerking their heads up and thrashing from side to side.

Adult butterflies, such as mourning cloaks (*Nymphalis antiopa*) and wood nymphs (*Cercyonis*), sometimes play possum, feigning death to fool a predator. And a few species make a noise: the European peacock creates a hissing sound by rubbing its fore- and hindwings together, scaring birds that apparently associate the sound with snakes; South American *Hamadryas* make a loud rattling or clicking noise when abruptly taking flight; and pupae of Oriental skippers (*Gangara*) and the small postman produce hisses and faint squeaks.

Some butterflies emit an unpleasant odor that may deter enemies. Female *Speyeria, Boloria,* *Limenitis,* and *Papilio* emit "disagreeable odors when pinched," and *Heliconius* butterflies are known for their "acrid odor," detectable from some distance, says field guide pioneer Alexander Klots.

Finally, there are the chemical defenses— toxins ingested by caterpillars, stored, and apparently passed along to the adults (or, in some cases, manufactured by adults). Among the best-known examples are the cardiac glycosides present in many, but not all, milkweed hostplants consumed by monarch caterpillars. Because different milkweed species have different levels of toxicity, adult monarchs vary in their toxicity levels. Even so, monarchs' vivid orange and black aposematic colors discourage predators sensitized by previous encounters with these butterflies.

Glasswing
Background colors visible through the transparent wing panels of glasswing, or clearwing, butterflies help to conceal the insect. When the angle of light turns the panels iridescent, the disruptive coloration also breaks up the outline of the butterfly's shape, as in the case of this *Greta oto* of Central America.

45

Common rose swallowtail
The common rose swallowtail (*Pachliopta aristolochiae*), widely distributed from India to Australia, exhibits red warning colors on its head and abdomen.

Common Mormon
The common Mormon butterfly *(Papilio polytes)* closely mimics the bad-tasting common rose swallowtail to protect itself from predators that confuse the two species—a classic example of Batesian mimicry.

After swallowing a monarch, many birds will vomit—and reject this species and its mimics in subsequent encounters. Environmentalists studying monarchs at their Mexican overwintering sites have discovered that blackheaded grosbeaks have developed immunity to toxins stored by monarchs, and that orioles and jays have become selective about which monarch body parts to consume. Like milkweed, passionflowers (*Passiflora*) bestow chemical protection upon caterpillars and adult butterflies; most passionflower vines (there are more than five hundred species) contain toxic cyanogenic glycosides and cyanohydrins and serve as hostplants for *Heliconius* species.

Postman

A postman butterfly (*Heliconius melpomene plesseni*) from Ecuador closely mimics the small postman (*Heliconius erato notabilis,* form *feyeri*) as part of a mimicry complex that protects both noxious species. Postman butterflies often fly with the small postman, although they shun direct sunlight.

Small postman

A small postman butterfly from Ecuador mimics postman butterflies in the same region. In Müllerian mimicry, both or all co-mimics are bad-tasting models, reinforcing the warning associated with their wing patterns and colors to predators that have survived a previous encounter with either butterfly. See the small postman species account for four other examples of this highly variable butterfly. Each subspecies is paired with an almost identical color morph of the postman butterfly, and there is near-perfect matching of geographic ranges between the corresponding regional color variations of the two species.

Courtship and Reproduction

"The mating biology of *Heliconius*," biologist Philip DeVries once observed wryly, "has some peculiar twists to it." As it happens, that characterization applies to more than just the longwings. Contrary to their demure image, many butterflies lead brazen sex lives, complete with aphrodisiacs, rough-and-tumble aerial takedowns, and multiple partners.

Finding a partner for breeding is arguably an adult butterfly's highest priority, and males employ one of two basic strategies: patrolling or perching. Patrollers reconnoiter likely habitats in their search for receptive females, inspecting movement and wing color and sometimes tracking by scent. Perching males, on the other hand, settle at one preferred site, often a rock or leaf, from which they rush out at passing insects, falling leaves, and other objects in hopes of encountering a receptive female. Perching males frequently exhibit "territorial" behavior, aggressively defending favored locales from rival males and sometimes confronting intruders by initiating upward spiral flights during which one ultimately retreats. Schappert recalls being attacked by "a crazed butterfly on a suicide mission"—a Northern pearly eye (*Enodia anthedon*)—that flapped its wings in his face every time he set foot in a wooded area between two fields.

Field researchers confirm that many species habitually mate in the same location: hilltops and gulch bottoms. "Hilltops are the butterfly equivalent of singles bars," declares Glassberg; males command a fine view from higher, open elevations, and unmated females regularly cruise nearby. Some scientists believe South American butterflies congregate in "leks"—swarms of males, commonly of more than one species—to secrete pheromones attractive to females.

Courtship behaviors vary considerably. Male orange-barred sulfurs (*Phoebis philea*), for example, "knock a female to the ground and mate with her within 15 to 30 seconds of her flying overhead," reports researcher John Feltwell. Other butterflies perform courtship dances, flying in zigzag patterns or hovering beside one another. Males release pheromones and many flutter their wings to waft the chemical perfume" toward a female; some pheromones make females receptive to mating, while others induce them to land. Pheromones are released from glands on the body that can be withdrawn to prevent evaporation. Some males (queens, for example) have hair pencils—eversible scent organs—which they dip into glands to gather pheromones. Flying ahead of and beneath a female, the male queen dusts the female's antennae with his scent; his pheromones have a compound, Scott reports, that "glues" the pheromone to her antennae and apparently discourages continued flight. Some hair pencils have a sweet aroma, while others smell rancid, DeVries reports; the common morpho's scent reminds some bystanders of vanilla.

Female heliconians have their own specialized organs, called "stink clubs." These abdominal lobes waft pheromones (perhaps chemicals that males transfer to virgin females) that act as anti-aphrodisiacs, repelling additional males with a rank odor.

Banded oranges
After courtship, a receptive female raises her wings to expose her abdomen while the male backs up his abdomen to make contact with her genitalia. This female banded orange (*Dryadula phaetusa*) from Costa Rica will mate only once during her brief lifetime, right after emerging from the chrysalis.

Clippers
From a distance, mating clipper butterflies (*Parthenos sylvia*) resemble a starfish. The male grasps the female's abdomen with claspers on his abdomen to engage the genitalia and transfers a spermatophore containing sperm and nutrients during copulation.

Courtship, of course, is a prelude; mating is the main event. "Butterflies are reproduction engines," Schappert declares. For some, copulation lasts about fifteen minutes; for others, up to twenty hours. Males can mate multiple times, as can most females, although female apollos (*Parnassias apollo*) usually mate only once. In a bold effort to ensure their own paternity, male tiger swallowtails, apollos, and others insert a plug (called a sphragis) into the female to block copulation with other males.

Unless a female adopts a rejection posture, the male will land beside her and curve his abdomen to the side, squeezing the end of her abdomen with his two claspers and inserting his penis. The male then transfers a spermatophore (a packet of sperm and nutrients) to the female, which she stores until depositing the eggs on a hostplant, at which

time the eggs are finally fertilized. Among monarchs, however, the mating process is different. "The male simply attacks the female on the wing, drives her to the ground and wrestles with her," says Pyle. "He will maneuver the female onto her back, wings spread, and cover her—a face-to-face embrace I've never seen among other butterflies."

If a pair of butterflies is disturbed while mating, "one individual flies off carrying the other dangling beneath," says Scott; in some species the male flies, in others the female. Male monarchs and their relatives carry the female on a "postnuptial flight," often to a nearby tree, where they remain for several hours or all night long.

One of the more "peculiar" behaviors among heliconians alluded to by DeVries is pupal mating. Male zebra and other longwings inspect passionflower vines regularly and recognize the scent of female pupae. They sometimes swarm over a pupa and compete to insert their genitalia "up to a day before she emerges," Schappert reports, in what he calls "the butterfly equivalent of rape."

Like snakes and other animals, butterflies are occasionally alleged to engage in "homosexual" behavior. Pyle has witnessed male queens engage in "impressive homoerotic behavior" in Florida, perhaps excited by alkaloids in vines whose nectar they were imbibing at the time. Generally speaking, however, male-male couplings are courtship "mistakes," declares authority Darryl Gwynne, "simply an effect of poor sex recognition," due to strong selective pressure on males to mate frequently and "mount any object that resembles a female."

Metamorphosis

"There is no 'beginning' in a butterfly's metamorphosis," Matthew Douglas writes in *The Lives of Butterflies*. "After all, a cycle is a cycle." The butterfly's life cycle consists of four stages—egg, caterpillar (or larva), chrysalis (pupa), and adult—during which a multi-segmented worm-like creature magically transforms itself into a stylish navigator of the skies.

After butterflies mate, the female searches for suitable (i.e., edible) hostplants on which to lay her eggs. Most attach their eggs singly to the underside of a leaf (one per leaf or one per plant), but some lay eggs in clusters or towers, and others deposit eggs on the leaf's upperside or near the hostplant. The size and color of eggs vary according to species; close inspection reveals a remarkable range of shapes, from miniature barrels, spindles, and spheres to odd lampshade-, pie-, and Frisbee-shaped forms. Eggs are generally pale green, cream, or white, but they change

The complex re-creation of the body of a caterpillar into the body and wings of a butterfly is, without doubt, one of the wonders of life on Earth.

—Phil Schappert,
A World for Butterflies (2000)

Great Mormon
A female great Mormon butterfly (*Papilio memnon*) lays eggs on the underside of a citrus tree leaf.

Tawny emperor eggs
Eggs of a tawny emperor (*Asterocampa clyton*) are laid in a large cluster on a hackberry leaf, providing safety in numbers. When the larvae hatch, they feed communally.

Monarch caterpillar
A just-emerged monarch caterpillar (*Danaus plexippus*) eats its own eggshell, a source of instant nutrition.

The caterpillar can weave around itself a new dwelling place with marvelous artifice and fine workmanship. Afterwards it emerges from this housing with lovely painted wings on which it rises heavenward.

—Leonardo da Vinci

color as they age—usually darkening—and some are conspicuously bright or boldly patterned to advertise their unpalatability. Most eggs hatch in seven to fourteen days, but others require weeks or months, and a few species overwinter as eggs.

If a hostplant's chemical or physical defenses are ineffective against the hungry hatchlings, each caterpillar—which Douglas characterizes as "a food-processing machine of formidable capacity" and Russell calls "a mouth attached to a stomach"—will increase exponentially in size and weight, necessitating successive molts of the outer skin. (Some caterpillars gain as much as 3,300 times their original weight, Schappert reports.) Most larvae will molt five times, although some tropical species shed their skins four to seven times and metalmarks up to nine.

Besides the standard six legs, each caterpillar has ten additional prolegs equipped with hooks (also called crochets) to assist with its distinctive crawling movement, an extending and shortening of the abdominal segments. Since a caterpillar has "small use for eyes or antennae," entomologist Robert Snodgrass asserts, "these organs are but little developed." But its jaws are strong and its long digestive tract well-designed to satisfy an enormous appetite. Many larvae possess a daunting arsenal of setae, horns, spines, antlers, and other appendages, some of them distasteful or able to sting predators. Swallowtail larvae may also evert fleshy red, yellow, or orange retractable tentacles, called osmeteria, which resemble the forked tongue of a snake and release a strong odor.

While larvae of some species are referred to as "gregarious," since they share leaves or plants with their kin, their behavior is not necessarily cordial. Many emergent caterpillars consume their own eggshell to reap a quick nutritional boost, and some inadvertently devour eggs containing their unhatched brethren.

The intervals between molts are known as instars; during each stage, the larval "eating machine" grows recognizably larger and may differ significantly in color and markings. Before the final molt, the caterpillar initiates a wandering phase, then settles down to spin silk (usually embedded with hooks, called the cremaster) from glands in the lower lip; this silk pad anchors the larva to a twig or other surface. Then the biochemical transformation to a chrysalis begins. This shell—soft at first but soon hardening—protects the larval body inside during its chemical dissolution and metamorphosis into an adult butterfly.

Chrysalides vary in appearance according to species, and some secure their hanging position by spinning a U-shaped silk girdle, "kind of like an electrical worker's safety harness," Schappert explains. Generally cryptic in coloration, the chrysalis is suspended for about four to fourteen days, though if subjected to harsh environmental conditions some safely remain in the pupal stage for several years. During this period, the chrysalis may sway or wriggle from time to time, and some species produce chirping, clicking, or humming sounds by rubbing their abdominal segments together. A butterfly emerges from its chrysalis with a swollen body full of fluid, pumps the fluid into the veins in

A monarch caterpillar hangs in a J-shaped position from a silk pad attached to a stem, preparing to pupate.

The last stage, or instar, of a caterpillar sheds its larval skin, revealing the soft chrysalis underneath.

After the final molt, the monarch's newly exposed chrysalis begins to harden.

The monarch's hardened emerald green chrysalis glistens in the sunlight, partially ringed by a row of gold dots and a black band.

The chrysalis turns transparent, and the adult developing inside becomes visible.

The bright orange wings and other body parts of the adult monarch are clearly visible an hour or two before the butterfly emerges.

The adult butterfly swallows air through spiracles, then expands its body to split the pupal shell along the length of the proboscis.

Hanging from the pupal shell, the monarch pumps fluid from its body into the veins of its soft wings, causing them to expand.

Once fully expanded, the monarch's wings must dry for several hours before the adult can take flight.

Zebra swallowtail caterpillar
A zebra swallowtail caterpillar (*Eurytides marcellus*) suspends itself from a pawpaw leaf with a silk girdle as it begins to form a chrysalis.

its wings fairly quickly, then excretes the stored waste products (meconium), which are usually reddish and watery. Swallowtails and sulphurs, whose chrysalides are supported by silk girdles, "pop the top of the chrysalis and walk out and up the branch quite quickly," Schappert continues. Butterflies that hang in a J-position as caterpillars—such as monarchs, Gulf fritillaries, and morphos—drop out of the chrysalis and emerge quickly. They then pause for a brief rest, Kenney explains, before reversing position to hang from the chrysalis while they pump their wings full of fluid—usually at night.

How butterfly wings go through this transition, scientists say, still involves considerable mystery. If researchers could copy the process, Hook suggests, engineers might be able to design larger solar panels for satellites, which could fold up more efficiently. As a result, the satellite signals to millions of cell phones and televisions in the future, he concludes, "may depend on the engineering of a butterfly wing."

Thermoregulation

Like lizards and snakes (and some tan-obsessed humans), butterflies are inveterate sunbathers. But unlike their warm-blooded, or endothermic, animal counterparts, butterflies have no internal mechanism to maintain a constant body temperature. Consequently, they depend almost exclusively on solar radiation to warm their environment sufficiently to permit flight. Butterflies seldom leave a perch until the ambient temperature reaches 55 degrees Fahrenheit (13° C), and scientists

say the optimal body temperature for flight is 82 to 100 degrees Fahrenheit (28° to 38° C). They can fly when the air temperature is between 60 and 108 degrees Fahrenheit (16° and 42° C), Scott reports, but their behavior is often "aberrant" at the two extremes.

To regulate their flight-muscle temperatures, butterflies bask in the sun or "hug the ground" to absorb heat reflected from rocks and soil. The most common thermoregulatory tactic is called dorsal basking: the butterfly spreads its wings wide open, exposing its body to direct sunlight. Another pose, known as lateral basking, involves closing the wings over the body, shifting the body broadside to the sun, and exposing the underside of the wings. In a third stance, called body basking, the butterfly angles its wings so that the thorax and abdomen receive maximum

American painted lady
Like other insects, butterflies depend primarily on solar radiation to regulate internal body temperature. This American painted lady (*Vanessa virginiensis*) basks with its wings fully open for maximum exposure to the sun's rays.

Cloudless sulphur
All butterflies are ectothermic, their bodies warmed or cooled depending on the ambient temperature. This cloudless sulphur butterfly (*Phoebis sennae*) is engaged in lateral basking, orienting the underside of its closed wings and leaning away from the sun while exposing as much of the body to the sun as possible.

exposure to the sun. When ground hugging, a butterfly absorbs heat on both sides of its wings and sometimes faces away from the sun, raising its head and thorax to soak up the sunlight.

If, after riding out a cold night in a sheltered area, a butterfly needs to move to a site in more direct sunshine, it may shiver its wings slightly, generating enough heat to warm its thoracic muscles. Species with darker colors have an advantage because they can absorb solar rays more quickly, just as those with lighter-colored wings can reflect heat. Researchers have found that butterflies in the Arctic and other frigid habitats can survive astonishingly low temperatures. Hibernating butterflies, Brewer reports, can withstand extreme cold at 20 degrees below zero Fahrenheit (-29° C), sometimes lower. Some caterpillars adapted to cold can survive being covered by freezing water, and chrysalides can survive 6-foot (1.8-m) snowdrifts. For monarchs and other species that cannot tolerate severe cold, the solution is to migrate to warmer climes.

In the tropics, butterflies may face a different problem: extreme heat. Their options are to be active early or late in the day, to frequent shaded areas and cooler forest canopies, and, when at rest, to fold their wings over their body to minimize exposure to the sun.

Hibernation and Aestivation

Hibernation, or overwintering, refers to a state of dormancy in which animals endure a period of cold temperatures; conversely, aestivation is a period of dormancy during excessive heat or drought. Depending on the climate and environmental conditions, butterflies utilize both states—although their dormant period is not a "true" hibernation like that of many mammals.

Butterflies can enter a period of dormancy in any one of their four stages of development—egg, larva, pupa, or adult—and the intensity and duration of their inactivity governs whether it is "quiescence" (a period of short duration) or "diapause" (an extended period of metabolic suppression and developmental arrest). For a particular species, dormancy typically occurs in only one stage; however, butterfly populations inhabiting different regions or born later in the year may vary in their responses to conditions.

To survive the harshness of a British winter, for example, the Camberwell beauty (mourning cloak) overwinters as an adult; the marsh fritillary (*Eurodryas aurinia*), on the other hand, overwinters as a caterpillar. "During this period," Ford writes, "they are so dormant that their habitat can be flooded and they may remain for weeks under water without harm." In fact, he adds, the larvae and pupae of many species can be frozen for days in a block of ice and survive without injury.

Prior to the onset of diapause, an adult mourning cloak boosts its energy reserves by ingesting large quantities of nectar and tree sap, which it converts to fat and glycogen. Once temperatures drop below 50 degrees Fahrenheit (10° C) and the days become shorter, the butterfly finds a well-insulated hideaway, such as a tree, woodpile, stone wall, or garage, in which to spend the winter.

(If their evergreen sanctuary is chopped down for a Christmas tree, butterflies may startle their hosts by suddenly taking flight inside a warm house.) Larvae usually retreat under a leaf or rock, burrow into debris, or wedge among grass.

If an adult's overwintering niche is too well-shielded, spring sunlight may not penetrate adequately. Since sunlight is required to warm a butterfly's wings sufficiently for it to fly, a shivering mechanism called muscular thermogenesis now kicks in, Douglas explains. Synchronous contraction and relaxation of thoracic muscles permit the wings to vibrate, raising the temperature high enough to permit the leg muscles to function. This allows the adult to move out of its tight quarters into the sunlight.

Some species, such as monarchs, migrate thousands of miles to overwintering sites; others disperse locally to nearby shrubs, trees, or leaf litter. Like amphibians and certain other animals, butterflies will aestivate if necessary, enhancing their survival odds by minimizing the risk of desiccation. This summer diapause during arid conditions ensures resumption of the life cycle during a more favorable season. Caterpillars will sometimes enter their chrysalis stage when faced with drought conditions. The resulting adults will be perfectly formed but smaller than average.

Migration

"Monarchs were everywhere," Annie Dillard wrote in her memoir *Pilgrim at Tinker Creek*, describing an unforgettable October day in the Blue

Monarchs
North American monarchs (*Danaus plexippus*) festoon the fir trees at overwintering sites in central Mexico after their spectacular southern migrations every fall. In the spring, they will fly northward in huge swarms.

Ridge Mountains of Virginia. "They skittered and bobbed, rested in the air, lolled on the dust—but with none of their usual insouciance. They had but one unwearying thought: South....They appeared as Indian horsemen appear in movies: first dotted, then massed, silent, at the top of a hill." Dillard was witnessing an annual fall migration in the early 1970s—before scientists even knew for sure *where* these insects were going.

Fall migrations of monarchs had been observed in North America for at least two centuries, but, unlike migrations west of the Rockies that terminated in roost sites along the California coast, the destinations of most of these Eastern flyers remained unknown. Then in 1975, an American engineer discovered the monarchs' winter sanctuary high in the Transvolcanic Range of central Mexico. The journey for some of these butterflies was 1,860 miles (3,000 km) or more, and, as the engineer stared at the millions of butterflies overhead, he noticed that cars were slipping and sliding on the blacktop where masses of exhausted monarchs fell. They were about to winter en masse in the same oyamel fir and cypress forests where their ancestors had; in the spring, they would mate, deposit eggs on milkweed on their journey north-ward, and ultimately die. But their offspring would press on, some as far north as Canada, leapfrogging in stages that might involve up to four generations before their return to Mexico in the fall. "No single butterfly," nature writer Sue Halpern notes, "ever makes the round trip."

Monarchs aren't the only butterflies to migrate: painted ladies (*Vanessa cardui*), red admirals (*Vanessa atalanta*), cloudless sulphurs (*Phoebis sennae*), great Southern whites (*Ascia monuste*), and long-tailed skippers (*Urbanus proteus*) are other known migrants, filling the sky with huge living clouds—sometimes for days—when their populations explode. Other butterflies migrate, too, but generally not en masse or such spectacular distances. Most seasonal migrations are on a "relatively small scale," authority Hugh Dingle reports, covering distances of only a few hundred or thousand meters. Insects migrate to escape deteriorating environmental conditions, he explains, or to colonize new habitats, or to take refuge in overwintering sites.

How migrating monarchs endure such long, taxing flights, and how they orient themselves to find Mexican forests they have never seen, are questions that intrigue scientists. University of Toronto biologist and glider pilot David Gibo, who has studied butterfly flight tactics extensively, has demonstrated that monarchs—"who apparently haven't the good sense to recognize their serious design flaws"—cannot possibly flap their wings all the way to Mexico. In his own fixed-wing airplane, Gibo remains in the air for extended periods by taking advantage of updrafts, and he has established that monarchs do the same. Monarchs spend a good deal of time gliding (traveling "nonpowered" in still air) and soaring (traveling via moving air), he concludes, to conserve energy and minimize wear and tear on their wings.

Geographically orienting themselves to arrive at the correct destination poses yet another challenge. Like birds, monarchs apparently use a "sun compass," and perhaps a magnetic compass, to accomplish this task.

Experiments by researcher Sandra Perez and others suggest that some butterflies "time-compensate" for the movement of the sun across the sky with a biological clock of their own, shifting their direction relative to the position of the sun. Perez's experiments with magnetism suggest that monarchs also navigate long distances with an internal geomagnetic compass sensitive to magnetic cues.

Seasonal winds and other meteorological conditions affect migration, too, just as hurricanes can relocate species to new geographical locales. Natural features such as mountain ranges, rivers, and coastlines are believed to be valuable landmarks. Some butterflies follow "unnatural" features as well, "sailing high above New York City's traffic-clogged skyscraper canyons," notes Glassberg, and highways often provide travel corridors. These migrants can be single-minded in their resolve: witnesses have seen streams of butterflies enter a window and continue flying forward until they reach an open window on the opposite side of the house and make their exit.

Whether the migrants are monarchs, painted ladies, sulphurs, or others, the sight of thousands or millions of these pilgrims sweeping the sky is a memorable one. "This spectacle," monarch authority Lincoln Brower once declared, "is a treasure comparable to the finest works of art that our world culture has produced over the past 4,000 years."

Predation and Parasitism

"From the viewpoint of their predators," Ken and Rod Preston-Mafham insist, "the larvae, pupae and adults of butterflies are merely a

convenient way of packaging food." No doubt about it: all stages of butterflies have natural enemies, and predatory fauna, parasitoids, and pathogens can have a significant impact on individuals and populations.

Fortunately, adult butterflies can "dodge and outmaneuver most vertebrate predators," affirms Douglas, "including frogs, toads, lizards, and, of course, lepidopterists"—except for certain birds and bats. Bird predation is difficult to verify, but mimicry studies have assessed beak-mark damage to butterfly wings, and surveillance of overwintering monarchs in Mexico reveals heavy predation by orioles, grosbeaks, and tanagers that have devised ingenious ways to avoid—or have developed resistance to—monarchs' noxious chemicals.

Mantid preying on sulphur
A predatory Chinese mantid devours a sulphur butterfly at a floral stakeout.

Lizards and, to a lesser extent, frogs and toads have been observed eating butterflies (although tree frogs and fence lizards, among others, can be quick to spit out distasteful or poisonous insects). Other predatory vertebrates such as monkeys are known to eat adults, and mice, shrews, snakes, and even foxes and bears hunt for and consume caterpillars.

But it is the invertebrates that exact the greatest toll. Mantids, robber flies, dragonflies, lacewings, ambush bugs, stink bugs, katydids, assassin bugs, and various beetles have all been observed attacking and eating butterflies (adults or caterpillars), some on

the fly and others bushwhacking their victims at floral stakeouts. Paper wasps are another threat, chopping up caterpillars "into easily carried chunks of protein as deftly as your local butcher carves sirloin steaks," Kenney observes. Orb-weaver spiders are the more visible villains, their webs entangling the wings of butterflies, although wolf, crab, and jumping spiders take their share of unsuspecting adults.

Unlike a predator, which kills its victim straightaway, a parasite weakens its host— "because its own fate is tied to the survival of the host," notes DeVries—depositing eggs inside or on the insect. Since an older

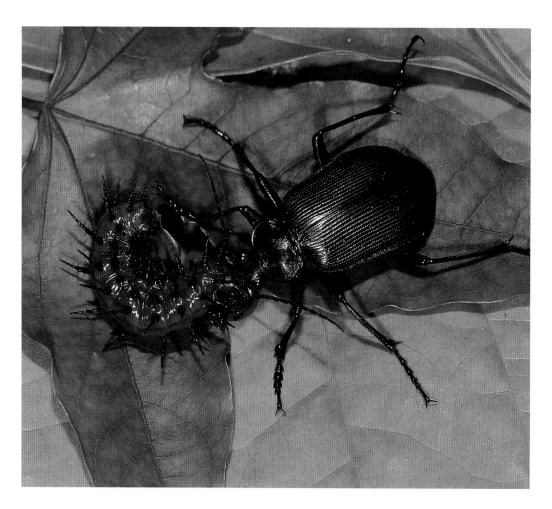

Beetle preying on Gulf fritillary caterpillar
Butterfly larvae fall prey to many predators. This Gulf fritillary caterpillar (*Agraulis vanillae*), despite its bright aposematic colors warning of toxins ingested from passionflower hostplants, has been attacked by a caterpillar hunter beetle. Other insects are often immune to the toxins that protect bad-tasting butterflies and their larvae from vertebrate predators.

Spider preying on zebra longwing
Spiders such as this black and yellow argiope prey heavily on butterflies, snaring zebra longwings (*Heliconius charitonius*) and other species in webs spun near host-plants and nectar sources.

caterpillar's spines or dense hairs may deter parasites, the egg-laying wasps and flies often prefer to penetrate the cuticle of newly hatched larvae or fresh pupae. At first, the larval parasitoids—the organisms that develop within the body of the host insect— feed on bodily fluids, but sooner or later they consume the internal organs. According to Scott, some flies lay tiny eggs on hostplant leaves, and after they are "inadvertently" eaten by the caterpillar, they proceed to grow inside the host.

Ants, on the other hand, are sometimes "enlisted" by blues, hairstreaks, and harvesters in some parts of the world for protection against arthropod predators and parasites, David Wagner and other researchers report. The ants carry butterfly larvae into their colonies and defend them from parasitic wasps; in return, the ants are permitted to "milk" precious honeydew produced by the butterfly larvae.

In addition to predators and parasites, disease-causing pathogens such as viruses, fungi, and bacteria are also responsible for butterfly mortality. These pathogens can be highly contagious and are particularly dangerous when they infect insect larvae that share crowded conditions.

During my excursions with a new best friend, Ellis MacLeod…, I acquired a passion for butterflies. Using homemade nets made of broomsticks, coat hangers, & cheesecloth bags, we captured our first red admirals & great spangled fritillaries & sought the elusive mourning cloak…. We decided we would devote our lives to entomology.

—E. O. Wilson, *Naturalist* (1995)

Chapter 3

Species Accounts

Families and Species

During the Middle Ages, moths and butterflies were swept into a convenient hodgepodge with other abundant insects and called "vermes"—the forerunner of today's vermin. Centuries ago, naturalists believed moths were "nighttime butterflies" and lumped both into a single catch-all group. Eventually, scientists made a further distinction between butterflies and moths, although they still assigned both to the order Lepidoptera. Of the international Lepidoptera Taxome Project's estimated 180,000 species of Lepidoptera, only about 17,950 species are butterflies. The rest are moths.

Today, butterflies are customarily divided into two superfamilies—true butterflies (Papilionoidea) and skippers (Hesperioridea). Traditionally, the two principal butterfly superfamilies have been divided into about eleven families: the swallowtails (Papilionidea); whites and sulphurs (Pieridae); gossamer-wings (Lycaenidae); metalmarks (Riodinidae); brush-footed butterflies (Nymphalidae); snouts (Libytheidae); milkweed butterflies (Danaidae); satyrs and wood nymphs (Satyridae); heliconians (Heliconiidae); true skippers (Hesperiidae); and giant-skippers (Megathymidae). Many authorities recognize as few as four or five of these families, and some recognize as many as fifteen.

Classification of butterfly families and species was once heavily influenced by their color and size, but today DNA analysis and microscopic examination of genitalia produce finer distinctions. "Butterflies are probably the most studied group of insects in the world," DeVries concludes, "but, oddly enough, their overall classification is still unresolved."

The distribution of these organisms is quite astonishing: butterflies are found on every continent except Antarctica, inhabiting every imaginable area except within a few degrees of the North and South Poles, extremely arid deserts, and alpine heights over 18,000 feet (5,500 m). Their distribution is influenced chiefly by climate and the ongoing availability of hostplants and nectar sources. More species of butterflies inhabit the American tropics than any other region of the world.

Red and blue cattleheart
Butterflies number roughly 18,000 species and are among the most studied insects on Earth. This red and blue cattleheart (*Parides photinus*), a relatively common inhabitant of Neotropical forests from Mexico to Costa Rica, belongs to the swallowtail family, although there is barely a suggestion of tails on its hindwings.

Cecropia moth
Moths such as this cecropia moth (*Hylaophora cecropia*) are generally distinguished from butterflies by their large feathered antennae, stouter bodies, furry-looking scales, and nocturnal behavior. Most butterflies have clubbed tips on their antennae and are active by day.

Giant swallowtail

Heraclides [Papilio] cresphontes

The giant swallowtail, frequently cited as North America's largest butterfly, has an imposing wingspan of 4 to 6¼ inches (10.2 to 15.4 cm). Distinctive rows of yellow spots cross its dark chocolate-brown or black upperside in an "X" formation and run down the wing margins, ending in a blob on the tip of each spoon-shaped wing tail. The underside is pale yellow or cream-colored with red-and-blue markings and dark trim.

Ranging from northern South America and the Caribbean throughout the southeastern United States and, rarely, to southern Canada, the giant swallowtail apparently orig-

inated in the tropics, where its larvae thrive on citrus. "Obviously, no citrus can grow here" in Kansas (or other central states), naturalist William Howe once remarked, but the giant swallowtail solved that problem by adapting to alternate hosts: prickly ash, hop tree, and rue.

In 1971, Californians were alarmed to discover giant swallowtail larvae on citrus trees in the San Joaquin Valley; the butterflies had apparently crossed the desert to the state's orange groves after hopscotching their way from Mexico to ornamental sour orange hostplants in Arizona. Eradication programs currently manage these troublesome strays.

The brown-and-white-blotched caterpillars, which naturalist Will Barker calls " undoubtedly one of the ugliest of all butterfly larvae," resemble bird droppings. Until, that is, they abruptly extrude a forked pair of long orange osmeteria that release "a stench that renders its immediate neighborhood quite uninhabitable by man or bird," entomologist John Henry Comstock once declared. Minno, however, demurs: "The smell is both pungent sweet and sour but not really foul." Ants and other would-be predators are sometimes smeared with the fluid from the so-called "stink glands" on the osmeteria, whose bright color may have prompted Florida citrus growers to nickname this agricultural pest the "orange dog."

Adult giant swallowtails prefer the bright sunshine of open clearings, glades, and fields near woodlands and streams, and frequently visit suburban gardens and roadsides where wildflowers grow. Males patrol in search of females, which lay orange,

Colombia; the king swallowtail ranges from Texas through Central and South America, Cuba, Jamaica, and Trinidad.
Giant swallowtail
The pattern of bright yellow spots on the uppersides

Giant swallowtail

The giant swallowtail has massive wings and is one of North America's largest butterflies. Distinctive rows of bright yellow spots on its dark chocolate-brown wings, in addition to a leisurely manner of gliding, make identification easy in most of the United States. In Texas, Mexico, and other points south, the story is different because the giant swallowtail's range overlaps with that of the nearly identical king swallowtail (*Papilio thoas*). The giant swallowtail ranges from Canada to Panama and Colombia; the king swallowtail ranges from Texas through Central and South America, Cuba, Jamaica, and Trinidad.

amber-brown, yellow, or light-green eggs singly on the tips of leaves. The chrysalis is a mottled gray or greenish brown and, when supported by a silk girdle from a tree, resembles a twig or branch. Adults commonly nectar on orange blossoms, honeysuckle, and lantana, and also sip juices from manure.

Like most swallowtails, the giant swallowtail usually flies 4 to 8 feet (1.2 to 2.4 m) above the ground but may wheel and swoop even higher. When nectaring, it flutters its wings continuously "much like a hummingbird," Florida entomologist Jaret Daniels states, although the wingbeats are nowhere near as rapid. Similar species include the Thoas swallowtail (*Papilio thoas*), Schaus' swallowtail (*P. aristodemus*), and Bahamian swallowtail (*P. andraemon*).

Eastern tiger swallowtail

Pterourus [Papilio] glaucus

The Eastern tiger swallowtail—the first American butterfly drawn by an artist and sent back to the curious citizens of England—is one of North America's most recognizable species, distinguished by its black tigerlike stripes on a yellow background. Curiously, in the South, as many as half the tiger females are almost completely black, mimicking the distasteful pipevine swallowtail (*Battus philenor*); shadows of their stripes, however, are still faintly visible. Very rarely, a genetic mix-up produces a gynandromorph half-male and half-female—with one striped yellow wing and one black wing, or an even rarer "mosaic" with patches of male and female scattered around the individual.

With a formidable wingspan of 3¼ to 6½ inches (9.0 to 16.5 cm), this large butterfly is a strong flyer. Common throughout the United States east of the Rockies, it apparently moves locally rather than migrates. It is one of five recognized species of tigers. In 1901, naturalist Mary Dickerson characterized Eastern tiger swallowtails as "bold and careless fellows," and Comstock declared that it had a special weakness for tobacco smoke. When fishing in the Adirondacks, Comstock would smoke a cigar every day and watch tiger swallowtails flutter about him and settle on his forehead and shoulders "to enjoy to the utmost the luxury of a second-hand smoke."

Male tiger swallowtails are well-known mud-puddlers, congregating in damp areas to extract sodium, nitrogen, and other minerals from sand or mud (also manure and carrion). The female lays green eggs singly on the leaves of magnolia, wild cherry, tulip poplar, sweet bay, ash, cottonwood, sassafras, and other trees and shrubs in woodlands, near streams and rivers, or in orchards and gardens. The smooth, deep-green caterpillar is plump with small but prominent eyespots on an enlarged thorax, which Comstock likened to the head of "a wicked little green snake." Enhancing the resemblance are a pair of orange forked

Eastern tiger swallowtails
The subtle sexual dimorphism of Eastern tiger swallowtails is apparent when individuals of the opposite sex nectar together on the same plant. The female (top), missing one of its tails probably due to a predator attack, has more blue on its hindwings than the male (bottom).

Female Eastern tiger swallowtail
Where the two species occur together, a black color morph of the female Eastern tiger swallowtail often mimics the toxic pipevine swallowtail (*Battus philenor*). Where the pipevine swallowtail is rare or absent, normal yellow-colored female tigers predominate.

Palamedes swallowtail
Pterourus [Papilio] palamedes

The Palamedes swallowtail, one of many American swallowtails named after ancient Greeks (this one a clever but unlucky hero of the Trojan War), is a majestic inhabitant of Deep South swamps, hammocks, pine flatwoods, scrubs, and other forested wetland and upland communities. Dubbed by some admirers the "Great Swamp Thing," this butterfly has large black wings adorned with prominent yellow bands and marginal rows of yellow spots, with a span of 4⁷/₁₆ to 5½ inches (11.2 to 14.0 cm). The Palamedes swallowtail, spicebush swallowtail, black swallowtail, female black form of the Eastern tiger swallowtail, and red-spotted purple all mimic the distasteful pipevine swallowtail (*Battus philenor*). The prominent orange-and-blue spots set against a black field and the underside of these species make them difficult to tell apart at a glance. From the upperside, the differences in wing size, shape, and coloration are more obvious, but the similarity in appearance is still striking, particularly when the butterflies are only glimpsed in flight.

Also known as the laurel swallowtail, this butterfly lays its yellow-green eggs on leaves of bay (red, sweet, or silk) and possibly sassafras. The caterpillar, pale green above and reddish below, has an enlarged thorax and a pair of yellow osmeteria, usually hidden from view. Prominent eyespots of orange with a black pupil resemble the eyes of a snake or lizard. Some experts believe the larvae overwinter; others insist only the mottled-green chrysalis overwinters. Palamedes swallowtails range

horns that sway menacingly, resembling the tongue of a snake, while emitting a foul odor.

The caterpillar spins a silken carpet in a one-leaf tent, which is curled and bound by threads of silk to conceal the caterpillar within. The faded green or brown chrysalis, suspended from a twig with a silk loop over the body, will pass for a piece of rough bark and hibernate until late spring or early summer. Adult Eastern tiger swallowtails visit gardens regularly to nectar on butterfly bushes, lilacs, honeysuckle, bee balm, Oriental lilies, clover, and thistles.

along the Atlantic coastal plain from New Jersey through Florida and along the Gulf Coast to Mexico. Adults nectar on the blue flowers of pickerelweed in swampy areas and on azaleas, phlox, and loosestrife in gardens. Males regularly gather in "puddle clubs," sipping diluted salts from mud.

Palamedes swallowtails are slow, lazy flyers. Males patrol woods throughout the day in search of a mate and, when courting, fly about 2 feet (0.6 m) or closer above a female—sometimes bumping into her—attempting to entice her to land. Fluttering his wings, the male wafts pheromones from his scent scales to the female's antennae; these pheromones will stimulate a receptive female to land and accept the male. At night, Palamedes swallowtails roost high in trees, often oak and palmetto.

Palamedes swallowtail
Newly emerged from its chrysalis, a Palamedes swallowtail dries its wings while clasping a twig. The long tails on the hindwings act as targets, drawing a predator away from the more vulnerable head.

Red and blue cattleheart

Parides photinus

The red and blue cattleheart, also known as the pink or the red-spotted cattleheart, is a vividly marked Neotropical butterfly that ranges from southern Mexico to Costa Rica. Its name refers to a double row of cranberry-red or neon-pink spots that sharply contrast against the iridescent blue sheen of the hindwings. A low, slow flyer generally observed within a few feet of the ground unless harassed, this butterfly has a wingspan of about 2½ to 3¾ inches (6.5 to 9.5 cm).

Relatively common in tropical forests of Central America, this species prefers trails, road cuts, and margins of forests to open spaces. Males patrol sunlit borders and patches of flowers but, unlike most other swallowtails, are not attracted to damp sand, urine, or manure. Androconial scales in pouches on the inside of the male's hindwings transfer pheromones during courtship. Hovering over a female, the male flutters his wings to release the scales, then dips repeatedly after she has landed. After copulating, males often deposit a sphragis to block other males from inseminating the female; over time, the plug disintegrates.

Females lay orange waxy-coated eggs that Hamilton Tyler describes as being shaped like miniature mushrooms, with fluted caps on stems. The butterflies likely exploit the chemical toxins in pipevine hostplants as a defense against predators. In their early stages, larvae are orange red or maroon with red, white, or black tubercles; as they mature, they turn velvety black. Adults sip nectar from flowers in the impatiens and madder families and other shrubs and trees. Individuals of some species of *Parides* have been found carrying pollen balls in their coiled proboscis, but scientists do not know whether *Parides* can absorb nitrogen from the pollen.

Red and blue cattleheart
The red and blue cattleheart, a Neotropical species, displays two rows of vivid cranberry-red or neon-pink markings—spots and chevrons—set off against the iridescent blue sheen of its hindwings.

Green jay

Graphium agamemnon

The green jay, also known as the tailed jay, green-spotted triangle, or Agamemnon's kite, belongs to a large genus of tropical African and Asian kite swallowtails. This species, distributed widely from northern India to Australia and Papua New Guinea, is a stunning black butterfly with a fragmented band of apple-green spots on the upperside and less-distinct green spots and markings on a lilac-brown underside—colors and patterns that provide excellent camouflage against leafy backgrounds, especially in the dappled shade of their native forest. The green jay's wingspan ranges from 3³⁄₁₀ to 4 inches (8.5 to 10.0 cm), and the fragile "tails" on its hindwings are distinctly stubbier than those of most swallowtails.

Green jays chiefly inhabit rain forests and monsoon forests or semi-evergreen vine thickets. The adults are very swift flyers, descend-

Green jay
A swift-flying inhabitant of rain forests from India to Papua New Guinea, the green jay has a striking dorsal pattern that features rows of green spots, although its hindwing tails are quite stubby for a swallowtail.

Green jay
The green jay's fragmented pattern of apple-green spots on a lilac-brown underside provides excellent camouflage, especially against leafy backgrounds in dappled light.

ing from the rain forest canopy to nectar on lantana in sunny clearings and on flowering trees and shrubs along the forest margins. "They pause for only a few seconds at each flower, with wings constantly vibrating, before flying to the next," Australian butterfly expert Michael Braby observes.

Females lay pale-yellow eggs singly on the tender leaves of custard apple plants, sour sop, and magnolia; upon hatching, the caterpillars are yellow green or dark brown but eventually turn bright green and sport a bulging brown-humped thorax. Larvae feed on soft new growth and risk death if they consume older growth, Braby reports. Mature larvae have somewhat hairy black spines and a pair of long, mottled olive-green spiracles with black tips at the posterior. The chrysalis is smooth and a pale-bluish green and sports a long red-tipped spike at the head region.

Emerald swallowtail

Papilio palinurus

The emerald swallowtail is known, rather confusingly, by a host of common names, including the banded peacock (also the common name for *Anartia fatima*, a.k.a. the brown peacock), moss peacock, green-banded peacock, Burmese banded peacock, and others. Whatever its moniker, this handsome species is distinguished by dramatic iridescent green bands that mix with black on the upperside of the wings and end in a vivid red spot. The brown underside, speckled with tiny green spots, provides camouflage for the butterfly when at rest.

Ranging from the Malay Peninsula through Sumatra, Borneo, and the Philippines, the emerald swallowtail is characteristically

Emerald swallowtail
The iridescent green bands on the wings of an emerald swallowtail, or banded peacock, remind some observers of the flashy colors on a peacock's tail.

Emerald swallowtail
Unlike the showy upperside, the brown underside of the wings and speckling of dots allow the emerald swallowtail to disappear among dark woodland shadows.

a woodland butterfly, although it also nectars on flowers in gardens. The caterpillars feed on various species of citrus plants and repel intruders with foul-smelling forked osmeteria that extrude from the thorax. The adult emerald swallowtail has a wing-span of about 3 to 3½ inches (7.5 to 9.0 cm) and is a swift flyer. Butterfly expert Bernard D'Abrera recalls sighting this species only once—in a Malaysian jungle near Kuala Lumpur—despite many years of field work. His hopes for photographing or capturing the individual were dashed when it flew "far too quickly" out of sight, never to be seen again.

Lime swallowtail
Papilio demoleus

A widely distributed migrant throughout much of the Middle East and Indo-Australian region, the lime swallowtail derives its name not from its coloration (which is black and yellow, not green) but from its love of citrus. In Singapore, for example, many city residents cultivate the common lime as a garnish for local cuisine, and "anywhere there is a lime bush, it is quite likely one can find this butterfly nearby," a local observer reports. A Chinese photographer adds: "I have a tangerine plant growing in a pot, and the lime butterfly often lays eggs on it."

Alternately known as the checkered swallowtail, this species is distinctively patterned: black with yellow spots and checkered fringes on the upperside, and a reddish-brown eyespot on the inner margin of each hindwing. The underside is brownish black, with paler yellow spots. In spite of its name, this swallowtail has no tails at all.

Typically found in tropical forests, dry inland meadows and fields, orchards, and gardens, the lime swallowtail has a "very puzzling" distribution pattern, according to D'Abrera, "without apparent continuity" throughout large areas within the Asian and Australian regions. (Hook suggests this migratory species is simply taking advantage of the wide distribution of its foodplants.) With a wingspan of 3¼ to 4 inches (8 to 10 cm), this lowland species flies rapidly (20 to 23 feet, or 6 to 7 meters, per second), usually close to the ground. They migrate in a constant direction, generally in low den-

sites, and by late afternoon these butterflies settle in tussocks of grass, where they perch overnight. By day, they are often spotted in clusters at damp patches near puddles or billabongs, sipping from moist sand.

Lime swallowtails nectar on the purple or pink flowers of low-growing legumes such as peas and beans. Females lay spherical pale-yellow eggs singly on citrus leaves or emu foot, and when large numbers of larvae hatch and survive, they sometimes pose an economic threat to lime, lemon, and orange orchards. The caterpillars are originally dark brown with splotches of white, resembling bird droppings early on, but turn green with dark transverse bands in later instars. The well-camouflaged greenish-brown chrysalis is attached upright to the stem of a hostplant or nearby rock and shored up with a silken girdle.

Lime swallowtail
The lime swallowtail of Indo-Australia and the Middle East loves citrus. Residents of Singapore and other Asian cities who grow limes and tangerines in gardens or on apartment balconies report these butterflies regularly lay eggs on the leaves of their plants.

Cabbage white butterfly

Pieris rapae

Sometime during the year 1860, a cabbage white butterfly from Europe made its North American debut in Quebec, Canada, and began transforming an entire continent. "How it came no man knows; perhaps in a lot of cabbages imported from abroad," authority W. J. Holland wrote; "maybe a fertile female was brought over as a stowaway. At all events, it came." That one fateful intruder spawned a series of broods that spread to California by 1866, occupied "all of New England" by 1871, and inhabited the entire eastern United States by 1881. Today, this ubiquitous upstart reigns from coast to coast and causes millions of dollars of damage to cabbage and related crops. Besides North America and Europe, the cabbage white is now firmly established in Hawaii, Japan, Asia, Australia, New Zealand, North Africa, and Iceland.

Known abroad as the small white, this species has a wingspan of only 1¾ to 2¼ inches (4.5 to 5.8 cm). While it has been derided by some observers as uninspiring and ugly, Glassberg characterizes it as "one of the most graceful inhabitants of the air." On the upperside, its wings are dull white, tinged with yellow in the female. Black or gray tips are displayed on the male's forewings. The male also has two black spots on each forewing, while the female has two. In early spring, these dark markings are often reduced or absent.

The cabbage white can be found in almost any habitat, although it prefers weedy open spaces, yards and gardens, roadsides, agricultural areas, marshes, and lightly wooded landscapes. Males usually patrol near hostplants in search of a female, then spiral upward in pursuit. If a female is unreceptive, she will fold her wings and drop to the vegetation below in what authority Rick Mikula calls "the butterfly equivalent of a brush-off." She rejects persistent suitors by raising her abdomen into the air, making copulation virtually impossible.

The white or pale-yellow eggs, deposited singly on cabbage-family hostplants or nasturtiums, are fascinating in close-up: each resembles a tiny barrel and has an intricate pattern of twelve vertical ribs. The caterpillars are a bright velvety green with three narrow yellow stripes and very fine hairs; they bore into cabbages and also consume turnip, mustard, broccoli, kale, Brussels sprouts, watercress, radish, and collard leaves, ingesting oils that make them distasteful to birds. The chrysalis is brown, gray, or green, often precisely matching the color of its background. It overwinters attached to a twig, fence, or wall, supported by a silk thread.

When the adult butterfly emerges in early spring, it searches for flowering vegetation on which to nectar, preferring purple, blue, and yellow to other colors. "The only time we ever found it truly attractive," John and Anna Comstock recall, "was when we saw it flitting serenely down Broadway in New York City in nowise dismayed by the turmoil."

Butterflies, the aristocracy not of instinct but of dress.

—J. Henri Fabre, *The Insect World of J. Henri Fabre* (1961)

Cabbage white
Although the cabbage white is a small, innocuous-looking butterfly, this invader from Europe can cause serious economic damage to agricultural crops and gardens, where its bright green larvae consume leaves of cabbage, broccoli, lettuce, and various mustards.

Southern dogface
A Southern dogface begins its emergence from a blue-green chrysalis. Females lay their eggs on the underside of leaves and are especially partial to members of the pea family.

Southern dogface

Zerene cesonia

Many observers insist the wing markings of a Southern dogface resemble the mug of a dog (some say a poodle, others a spaniel). But not everyone agrees. "It is certainly a new species of dog," the Comstocks concluded more than half a century ago, adding that "it looks far more like a duck with bill opened in the act of quacking."

Both sexes are bright lemon yellow, with the suggestion of a dog's snout and prominent black "eyes" on the upperside of the forewings; seasonal variations display yellow on the hindwing undersides in the summer, a pink or burgundy blush in the winter. "It takes a sharp eye to pick out the 'dog face' pattern on its wings," Brian Cassie says. When the butterfly lands, it brings its wings together immediately and the dog image disappears. (A related species, the California dogface, is nicknamed the "flying pansy" because its wing colors and markings resemble a flower more than a canine; a Mexican species that strays across the border has been dubbed the "wolf-faced version.")

Abundant in the southern half of the United States and southward to Argentina, this sulphur butterfly is found along road-sides, near open woodlands, in fields, weedy pastures, and agricultural lands. It has a wingspan of 1⅞ to 2¹⁵⁄₁₆ inches (4.7 to 7.4 cm) and is a rapid flyer; it migrates from the South and has been observed in huge swarms in the Rio Grande Valley of Texas.

The male patrols by day and fans a prospective mate with his wings to transmit pheromones. Even a stationary female-like object can trigger a male's entire courtship sequence, researchers have discovered. His "mate-identification" requirements are so simple, it appears, that a male will even attempt to copulate with a paper facsimile.

Females lay white or pale-green eggs (which turn crimson) on false indigo, leadplant, clover, and other members of the pea family. The caterpillars are generally dull green, marked with yellow-and-black crossbands and yellow to orange lateral stripes; their bodies are covered with small black hairy tubercles. The chrysalis, usually blue- or yellow-green with pale streaks, overwinters in some areas, although the Southern dogface also hibernates as an adult. Adults sip nectar from purple clover, blazing star, and thistles, and also sip mud.

Southern dogface
Each forewing of a Southern dogface has an eyespot on a yellow pattern that suggests to some observers the profile of a poodle—although detractors claim it looks more like a duck.

Orange-barred sulphur

Phoebis philea

Entomologist W. J. Holland once referred to the orange-barred sulphur (a.k.a. the yellow apricot) as a "noble species" from a family of "showy" insects. A bar of deep orange is visible on the male's bright apricot-yellow forewings, along with an orange-red patch on the hindwing. The female, which is a bit larger than the male, is seasonally dimorphic: one form is yellow or yellow-orange, the other cream or off-white. Females have a central spot and scattered dark-brown spots on each forewing, with smoky-red patches on the borders of the hindwing. The average wingspan of this butterfly is 2¾ to 3⅞ inches (7.0 to 9.8 cm).

Orange-barred sulphur
The orange-barred sulphur exhibits sexual dimorphism. The larger female has black marks on its forewings; the smaller male has orange bands or bars on the forewings. Both sexes have a wide orange band on the hindwing.

The orange-barred sulphur is relatively common from southern Florida through Central America and South America as far south as Brazil and Peru. In the United States, it is something of a nomad, occasionally straying as far north as New York and Minnesota. This butterfly originally reached Florida from the West Indies around 1928. Emmel speculates that adults flew in or were blown in by a tropical storm; alternatively, their larvae may have been imported on nursery stock. The butterfly became a permanent resident when it discovered native legumes from its hostplant genus, *Cassia*, which grow wild in southern Florida.

Orange-barred sulphurs are frequently observed in city parks and gardens, open woodlands, along edges of tropical forests and pinelands, and flying through the streets of Central and South American cities. They are partial to open areas, whether pastures or above the forest canopy, and seem to thrive in areas disturbed by humans. Males congregate en masse at damp spots along riverbanks and are attracted to urine and sweat.

The orange-barred sulphur flies very fast and high—observers say it appears to bounce at times—in full sunshine during the hottest part of the day, descending from the heights to sip nectar from red and yellow flowers or to sip at mud. Descriptions of courtship suggest that males are fast in this endeavor as well. "A female flying overhead," DeVries reports, "may be intercepted by the male, bashed around in the air, forced to the ground, and be coupled to the male, all within 15 to 30 seconds." Ultraviolet-reflecting bars on the wings of males apparently play a

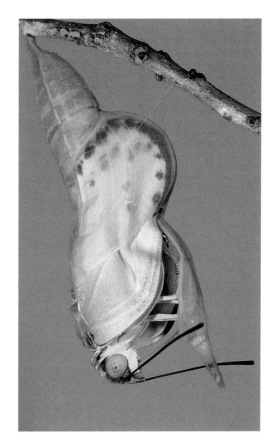

Orange-barred sulphur emerging
An orange-barred sulphur, with yellow wings and black spots distinctly visible, begins its emergence from the split chrysalis.

Orange-barred sulphur opening wings
The newly emerged orange-barred sulphur hangs onto its chrysalis and rests while its wings open and dry.

role in sexual and species discrimination, and androconial scales on the male's forewings secrete pheromones enticing to females.

Eggs are white, laid singly on leaves and flowers or flower clusters, and caterpillars often prefer the flowers to leaves. Caterpillars are yellow green with black tubercles and yellow bands, or green with orange patches and light bands. Researchers believe larvae that develop on cassia flowers become yellow, while those on foliage tend to be green. The chrysalis, which is generally some shade of green with a gray, blue, reddish, or purple-rose tint, has a keel and a tapered head.

Harvester

Feniseca tarquinius

While only one species of harvester is found in all of North America—compared to roughly fifty in Africa and Asia—this one small species boasts some very sizeable quirks. It is the only North American butterfly whose larvae are carnivores; adults do not feed on flower nectar; and the chrysalis bears a striking resemblance to a monkey's head.

The harvester acquired its name because the predatory larvae "harvest" woolly aphids, mealybugs, and other scale insects rather than munching on vegetation. (The species epithet, *tarquinius*, is derived from a Roman tyrant named Tarquin.) Adults remain near colonies of their insect hosts, Opler notes, and obtain their nutrition from the hosts' sugary secretions, called honeydew, on the leaves of trees—chiefly alders, beech, ash, and witch hazel. Caterpillars of some species apparently secrete their own honeydew to attract ants, which carry the caterpillars to their nests to protect them from predators, Glassberg reports. Adult harvesters are true mavericks: they don't sip nectar from flowers like most butterflies, and their proboscis is therefore much shorter. Besides honeydew, adults imbibe sap and sip moisture from mud, dung, and dead animals.

Harvesters vary considerably in color and pattern, from bright orange to dark brown on the upperside, with dark spots and borders. The mottled underside is pale brown, with irregular spots and delicate white or silver markings on the hindwings. Their wingspan is only about 1 to 1¼ inches (2.5 to 3.2 cm), and their flight is characterized as quick, erratic, and nervous.

The harvester is found in eastern North America from Maine and southern Canada west to North Dakota and south to Texas and Florida. Its habitat is primarily deciduous woodlands, especially near streams or wet areas where alders grow. Adults rest in open glades with their wings extended, sunning in the late afternoon. Males perch on leaves and wait for females, taking flight to patrol the area briefly before returning to a spot near their original perch.

Females select leaves or stems of plants infested with aphids and lay pale-green eggs singly among the woolly hosts; when they hatch, after just three or four days, the gray or greenish-brown caterpillars "start at once on their career of slaughter," devouring the aphids, the Comstocks remark. To avoid ants, the caterpillar weaves a silken covering that provides a safe retreat for molting. If an alder stem is jostled, the caterpillar may drop to the ground or lower itself a short distance by a silken thread—perhaps to save itself from angry ants, which attack any predator that interferes with their flock of honeydew-producing aphids.

Harvester chrysalis
The chrysalis of the harvester butterfly is notorious for its uncanny resemblance to the face or skull of a monkey. The ominous "eyes" likely protect the chrysalis by scaring off predators.

Harvester
North America's single species of harvester rests on a leaf. Rather than feed on flower nectar, adults eat honeydew secreted by aphids.

Harvester caterpillar
The harvester caterpillar is carnivorous and preys on colonies of woolly aphids.

The chrysalis, formed after an unusually short sequence of just three molts, is a mix of green and brown with irregular dark patches—and looks astonishingly like a miniature ape's head (or some say a serpent's). Ecologists Alexander and Elsie Klots once said it's a pity the chrysalis is so small (about ⅛ inch, or 0.3 cm), "for otherwise it would be a wonderful subject for speculation by overenthusiastic naturalists, who are always seeing fanciful resemblances to crocodiles, snakes, and owls in various insects, and then stating that these were developed for the purpose of frightening away birds."

Atala

Eumaeus atala

Once so scarce it hovered on the brink of extinction in North America, the atala, or coontie hairstreak, is a lucky lepidopteran. This small butterfly, which belongs to the distinctive hairstreak subfamily with hairlike tails on their hindwings and small streaks on the underside of their wings, was rescued by environmentalists, gardeners, and corporate partners who planted thousands of coontie plants in patches across southern Florida.

"This sensational animal is difficult to misidentify," says Glassberg, "except in flight, when it looks remarkably mothlike." Lacking the tails of its fellow hairstreaks, the atala has a distinctive red-orange abdomen and metallic blue or green scaling above on velvety black; three rows of iridescent aquamarine spots and a large red patch appear on the underside of black hindwings. The soft metallic iridescence of this butterfly gives it a bold, exotic look, but the red and other bright colors serve an important function: to warn off predators.

Atala

A male atala, or coontie hairstreak, nectars on blanketflower. This butterfly, spared from extirpation in Florida by the efforts of conservationists, flaunts a bright orange-red abdomen advertising toxicity acquired from its coontie hostplants.

Since the coontie hostplant is poisonous, the caterpillar, chrysalis, and adult forms are toxic as well.

Ranging from southern Florida to Cuba, the Bahamas, and West Indies, the atala favors subtropical hammocks and pinelands, edges of hardwood forests, and adjoining open areas, especially those with native and ornamental cycads, such as parks, botanical gardens, and suburban backyards. In Florida, colonies experienced significant population declines after widespread harvesting of coontie for arrowroot starch in the late nineteenth century and again after the great 1926 hurricane. When the atala later fell victim to Florida's real-estate boom and fires in the Everglades (by 1965, only one colony was known to survive), "dedicated conservationists provided coontie plants for the few remaining butterflies to lay their eggs and then moved the potted plants with the eggs to various locations to start new colonies," Emmel recounts in his book about Florida butterflies. Since about 1980, he adds, the species has made a "spectacular recovery."

The atala's wingspan averages 1½ to 2 inches (4.0 to 5.1 cm), and the flight of adults is slow and lazy-looking. Males perch on leaves and seldom stray from their colony, while females may fly short distances. Colonies roost in low-growing trees, where adults can sometimes be touched without being disturbed.

During courtship, males evert hair pencils at the tip of the abdomen and hover in front of females, wafting pheromones. Females lay clusters of white or grayish eggs on the new growth of hostplants. The caterpillars are bright red with two rows of prominent yellow spots on the back and dark hairy tubercles. These caterpillars are gregarious, feeding together in groups that make their bright warning colors even more obvious to deter potential predators. The chrysalis is usually reddish brown, and the yellow spots within are often visible through the outer shell.

Oak hairstreak
Fixsenia [Satyrium] favonius

The "correct" scientific classification of the oak, or Southern, or Southern oak hairstreak has been debated by taxonomists for years, and close inspection of the genus reveals why: this tiny butterfly is highly variable in color, and some populations intergrade with the Northern hairstreak. The result is what experts call a blend zone, where characteristics mingle and identification becomes extremely difficult.

Sporting two long tails on each hindwing, the oak hairstreak is dusky brown above and gray brown beneath, with orange-red patches and blue markings on the underside (more conspicuous in females). On the underside, both sexes have a white-bordered black line in the shape of a "W" and a broader line along the margin of the hindwing. Males have an oval cluster of gray scales on the upperside of the forewing, where pheromones are produced. The entire wingspan is only 1 to 1½ inches (2.5 to 2.8 cm).

Ranging from Massachusetts down the Atlantic coast through the Gulf States and west to Illinois and Oklahoma, the oak hairstreak favors woodland edges, power line cuts, oak hammocks, scrub oak forests,

Southern oak hairstreak
Perched on flowering lantana with wings closed, a Southern oak hairstreak displays long tails on its flamboyantly marked hindwings, mimicking its own head and antennae to deflect a predator's attack to the more dispensable rear wings.

and mixed pine-oak habitats. Adults nectar on flowers in meadows near oak woods or pine barrens, favoring white sweet clover, dogbane, and New Jersey tea. Males perch with wings closed above their back, Opler notes, and wait for receptive females to show up. After mating, females lay their pinkish-brown eggs singly on twigs near buds, typically those of Southern red, live, or blackjack oak; the eggs overwinter and hatch in the spring. The caterpillars are pale or yellow green with dark green-and-yellow stripes; they feed on the scaly catkins, buds, and leaves of host-plant oaks. The oak hairstreak's chrysalis is pale brown, dappled with black.

Little metalmark
Calephelis virginiensis

The metalmark butterflies, whose name derives from their metallic wing markings, have somewhat subdued colors in North America compared to those of their flashier relatives in the tropics; there, the subfamily "runs riot," declare Alexander and Elsie Klots, and some 1,300 species form "a completely bewildering mélange of pigmental and structural colors, patterns, and wing shapes that defies any generalizations."

One of eight scintillant metalmarks (there are an additional three checkered species) in the United States, the little metalmark is indeed tiny, with a wingspan of only ½ to 1 inch (1.2 to 2.5 mm). On the upperside, its wings are rusty orange brown, copper, or brick red, with a continuous silver-blue line and other broken lines or specks. The underside, a pale tawny color, has similar steely-blue lines and markings. Hairy dark-brown fringes border the fore- and hindwings. When sunlight strikes its wings, this diminutive butterfly rivals the exotic marvels in butterfly conservatories, glistening "as though its wings have been decorated with lines of tiny silver rivets," one field observer declares.

Ranging from extreme southeastern Virginia down the Atlantic coastal plain to Florida and across the Gulf States to southeastern

Little metalmark
Visible on both sides of the fringed rusty-orange wings of the little metalmark butterfly are metallic gold and blue-specked markings.

Texas, the little metalmark favors open grassy areas, open pinewood flats, salt-marsh meadows, wet saw grass prairies, and dry Everglades savannahs. Males commonly perch on or underneath leaves of low-growing plants, their wings spread as they watch for prospective mates. Females lay their eggs singly on leaves of yellow thistle; the sluglike caterpillars, generally pale green with reddish-brown blotches and rows of white hair tufts, rest on the underside of these leaves by day and consume them by night. The little metalmark's stout chrysalis is pale green as well. Adults nectar on short-flowered composites, including sneezeweed and herbs with blue blossoms, and on milkweeds. In 2001, the U.S. Postal Service issued a set of four stamps featuring carnivorous plants; the Venus flytrap's rather fiendish red "jaws" are depicted ensnaring a hapless little metalmark.

American snout

Libytheana carinenta

The snouts make up a subfamily of butterflies equipped with remarkable "noses," or, more accurately, labial palpi—peculiar appendages that flank the proboscis. Snouts are cosmopolitan butterflies found on every continent, although the American snout, known as Bachman's snout for many years, is the only U.S. resident. A native of the South, as well as Mexico, the West Indies, and northern South America, this species also migrates extensively throughout the United States.

Aside from the odd-looking schnoz, it is the migratory excursions that give the snout its notoriety. Over the last century, eyewit-nesses periodically have reported skies darkened by giant swarms of snouts. An estimated 25 million snouts per minute passed over a 250-mile expanse of Texas for eighteen days in September 1921, heading toward the Rio Grande River. This flight, entomologist Larry Gilbert calculates, may have involved as many as 6 billion butterflies. In 1978, Gilbert himself witnessed a great migration. "They clogged car radiators," Gilbert told Russell. "They ruined laundry. They passed overhead like a muddy, aerial river." In the Southwest, so many millions of American snouts are struck by vehicles that the slickened roads have to be routinely closed for safety, Glassberg notes.

Yet these awe-inspiring insects are ordinarily inauspicious. Their wingspan is only 1½ to 2 inches (3.8 to 5.1 cm), and their color is not at all flashy: dark brown above, with orange patches and white spots. The underside is either drab and dark or what the Comstocks characterize as "a beautiful vague pattern of sheeny, olive brown, and ashes of roses." The tips of the forewings are distinctively squared off or notched and almost look like they have been snipped with scissors.

The unusual pair of snoutlike palpi that jut forward from the head of this butterfly serve at least one recognizable function: they offer camouflage by mimicking the stems of dead leaves when the butterfly perches head-down on twigs. The snout's other physical curiosity—the male's forelegs are much smaller than those of females, whose normal-sized forelegs also have claws—has not been adequately explained.

The butterfly's habitats include scrublands, brushy fields, pastures, wooded swamps,

American snout

Snout butterflies, the Pinocchios of the butterfly world, project their prominent palpi for all to see. For camouflage, the underside of an American snout's wing resembles a dead leaf, and the long snout resembles a stem. The bright orange flash colors seen in this photo are normally hidden by the hindwing while the butterfly is at rest; when the butterfly feels threatened, it extends the forewing fully, revealing the hidden color just before flying away.

woodland edges, and riverbanks. Adults nectar on goldenrod, dogwood, raspberry, and other blossoms, and sometimes take sap from injured trees and sip on fruit. The flight of American snouts is rapid and low but somewhat erratic. Males tend to perch rather than patrol, and "mating seems to occur all day," Scott says. Females lay eggs singly on the underside of leaves of hackberry, sugarberry, or wolfberry hostplants. Caterpillars are highly variable in color, though generally a dark velvety green with yellow lateral stripes, many tiny pale spots, and two black spots. Individuals frequently arch their thorax and tuck their head down, Wagner notes, which explains why observers often report that the caterpillar has a "pronounced hump." The chrysalis is deep or bluish green, sometimes yellow green, with yellow dots and a sharply pointed head. In the South, adults are known to overwinter.

Monarch
Danaus plexippus

When the eminent butterfly authority Samuel Scudder coined the name "monarch" in 1877, he declared: "It is one of the largest of our butterflies, and rules a vast domain." That domain is now far more vast than Scudder ever could have imagined. Today, the monarch not only summers in southern Canada and throughout the entire continental United States, it also ranges south to Argentina, has colonized Bermuda, the Galapagos Islands, Hawaii, Australia, New Guinea, the Philippines, India, Java, and Sumatra, and has strayed (probably as a stowaway on ships) to England, Western Europe, Greece, and the occasional oil derrick at sea. That explains its other common name: the wanderer.

The monarch, Scott and others agree, is the world's most strongly migratory butterfly. Since 1937, data collected from tagged individuals confirm that monarchs can fly up to 200 miles (322 km) in a single day. The longest documented flight is 2,880 miles (4,635 km), a record cited by Monarch Watch for a Canadian monarch recaptured in Texas in the spring of 1989 after presumably overwintering in Mexico; the longest one-way record (Ontario to Mexico) is 1,870 miles (3,009 km). No other butterflies or moths are even close runners-up.

Thanks to its regally handsome orange-and-black wings, the monarch is recognizable around the globe; its "majestic pilgrimages" (John Steinbeck's characterization) are practically legendary, and the international press

Monarch
A monarch nectars on ixora. The male monarch has a dark-colored androconial pouch on each hindwing that stores pheromones; these sexual "perfumes" are wafted during courtship to attract a female and stimulate mating.

reports on the status and condition of overwintering colonies. The monarch even has its own court: the queen, which mimics the monarch but whose colors are "more root beer than orange juice," according to Pyle; and the viceroy, which mimics the queen but has a distinct black line across the hindwings. The monarch is larger than both, with a wingspan of 3⅜ to 4⅞ inches (8.6 to 12.5 cm), compared to the queen's 2¾ to 3⅞ inches (7.0 to 9.8 cm) and the viceroy's 2⅝ to 3⁵⁄₁₆ inches (6.7 to 8.5 cm).

Monarchs are closely identified with milkweed plants. Milkweed has multifold appeal: adult monarchs sip the nectar, which

is poisonous to vertebrates, and females lay their eggs on its leaves, stems, and flowers. After hatching, caterpillars ingest and store the toxins, making themselves and their adult forms highly unpalatable to most predators. Some seventy-five milkweed species grow in the United States alone, enticing monarchs farther and farther northward. These butterflies are tropical, however, and cannot survive subfreezing temperatures; consequently, northern migrants must retreat below the frost line each fall. Lincoln Brower, the dean of monarch authorities, hypothesizes that monarchs tracked the continental expansion and retraction of the milkweed

Monarchs
Monarchs mud-puddle on damp ground in Michoacán, Mexico, near the forests where they overwinter. Butterflies, usually males, draw sodium ions from the moisture to replenish their levels depleted during mating.

Monarch

Wings closed, a monarch nectars on a Mexican flamevine. The butterfly's intense aposematic colors warn predators that this species stores chemicals from toxic milkweed ingested by the larvae.

hosts' range during the Pleistocene Era. Natural selection, he explains, would have favored individuals that moved southward as summer drew to a close. Over time, the migration pattern became "increasingly sophisticated, ending in the present round-trip migration, one of the most complex in the animal kingdom."

Every year, millions of North American monarchs migrate southward in giant swarms— "the most spectacular mass movements of any insect," Pyle says. Monarchs born east of the Rockies fly, for the most part, to the forested slopes of Michoacán, Mexico, while those born west of the Rockies typically fly

to California's coast. But Pyle has witnessed firsthand, and wing tags have confirmed, that these two critical overwintering destinations are not entirely exclusive of each other's regional migrants, and most Americans probably do not realize that the monarchs that visit their gardens in the spring aren't the same ones that migrated south the previous fall— they're actually those monarchs' grandchildren or great-grandchildren.

In fact, prior to 1975, scientists weren't exactly sure where the giant swarms of monarchs from Canada and the Northeast, East, Southeast, and Midwest headed each fall. Traditionally, the Western migrants overwintered on California's Monterey Peninsula, where they massed in huge clusters on pine, cypress, and eucalyptus trees. The sheer weight of millions of butterflies can be staggering, however, and in late 2004 the city of Pacific Grove temporarily closed its world-famous sanctuary to the public after a tourist was killed by a pine branch that fell during the Monarch Madness Festival.

The winter destination of most eastern populations remained a mystery until researchers located the monarchs in oyamel firs at high altitudes west of Mexico City. Initial estimates suggested there were ten million monarchs per hectare (2.47-acre plots), but revised estimates suggested five times that number. By his calculation, Brower believes these fir trees can be festooned with as many as one billion monarchs.

Scientists wondered how these butterflies, which have about a nine-month life span and had never flown to Mexico before, managed to find the hidden mountain retreats. Experiments eventually suggested that monarchs use the sun and magnetic fields to navigate. They probably seek visual cues as well and may detect the scent of scales left behind by billions of their predecessors.

The stakes are extremely high for populations crowded into such small locales, and millions of monarchs were decimated in 1981 and 2002 by catastrophic winter storms. Persistent illegal logging and predation by birds take heavy tolls as well. Recent winter-colony estimates and spring-migration counts released by Monarch Watch have been discouraging, and scientists and butterfly enthusiasts alike are imploring officials in Mexico and the United States to do more to protect what Brower calls an "endangered phenomenon."

Monarchs themselves are a particularly charismatic species. In flight, these butterflies enthrall observers. Combining strong wing flapping with energy-efficient gliding and soaring on currents of wind, monarchs hold their wings open in a distinctive V-shaped position and sail over open fields and gardens, often following corridors such as roads and rivers, in search of nectar and hostplants. From tiny barrel-shaped eggs, usually cream-colored or greenish white, emerge caterpillars that are a dull creamy-white color with black heads. As they stoke themselves with milkweed leaves and store up the toxic glycosides, the caterpillars boldly advertise their unpalatability with vivid aposematic colors—gaudy rings of yellow, black, and white. The chrysalis is a soft emerald green, encircled with a gold-edged black band and adorned with yellow specks that assume a gold metallic gleam.

Adult males, it seems, have lost their knack for gallant courtship. They patrol near milkweed hostplants, and, according to Pyle, when a male spots a female, he forces her to the ground, maneuvers her onto her back, and covers her. After a succession of matings with other females, the male may become "less aggressive," he adds, "but the 'courtship' following the winter dormancy can only be considered ravishment."

Gradually it occurred to me, gradually it registered, that though there were millions of them, they were not leaves at all, they were butterflies, monarch butterflies, the butterflies of my backyard. They were in the air, and so heavy on the branches of the pine trees that the branches bent toward the ground, supplicants to gravity & mass & sheer enthusiasm....The clamor of butterfly wings was as constant & irregular as surf cresting over rocks.

—Sue Halpern, *Four Wings and a Prayer: Caught in the Mystery of the Monarch Butterfly* (2001)

Large tree nymph
As it sips nectar, a large tree nymph from Indonesia stretches its wings, which resemble delicate rice paper often used in the making of kites.

Large tree nymph
Idea leuconoe

The large tree nymph of Southeast Asia goes by several names, but two in particular—the paper kite and rice paper butterfly—evoke the manner in which this butterfly glides and floats like a kite constructed of thin rice paper. Some two dozen subspecies are distributed widely from southern China and Thailand throughout the Malay Peninsula, Philippines, and Taiwan, although habitat destruction on Java may have caused the butterfly's extirpation there.

The large tree nymph is easily identified by its imposing 3¾- to 4½-inch (9.5- to 10.8-cm) wingspan and its translucent grayish-white wings, which feature a bold mix of black veins, spots, and zigzag markings. The body is slender, like that of a damselfly or darner, and the wings, despite their paper-thin delicacy, are actually quite tough. The high ratio of wing size to body size is responsible for the butterfly's weak fluttery flight, which alternates with gliding and floating. The sudden appearance of a large tree nymph fluttering out of a forest on its ghostly wings has given rise to legends about this specterlike butterfly in many localities.

Adult large tree nymphs, generally associated with coastal mangrove swamps, tropical forests, and secondary woods, are attracted to a variety of flowers, including *Thunbergia*, heliotrope, buddleia, and oleander. Larval foodplants include the milkweeds *Parsonsia*, *Cynanchum*, and *Tylophora*.

Courtship behavior involves a male (sometimes several) fluttering with strong

Large tree nymphs
A pair of large tree nymphs mate on tropical vegetation, their translucent black and white wings obscuring the male's valvae clasping the female's abdomen while sperm are injected into her mating tube.

wingbeats above and slightly behind a female, to waft pheromones dispensed from hair pencils in her direction. When the female flies off, the male pursues her. After mating, the female lays her eggs on the leaves of milkweed hostplants, which presumably make larvae and adults distasteful to predators. (The adults are mimicked by the Asian swallowtail, *Graphium idaeoides*.) The caterpillars are velvety black, with narrow yellow bands, red spots, and four pairs of black filaments down the back.

Large tree nymph caterpillar
Attention-grabbing black and white bands accentuated by red spots warn predators that the larval stage of the large tree nymph, which eats poisonous milkweed hostplants, is distasteful.

Striped blue crow revealing iridescence
The wings of a female striped blue crow butterfly reveal the structural color blue when lit from a particular angle, suggesting a crow's plumage observed in direct sunlight. The sudden flash of iridescence may momentarily confuse a predator.

Striped blue crow lacking iridescence
The same female striped blue crow lit from a different angle lacks blue iridescence and instead appears black with the customary white spotting and stripes. The male has the same spots and iridescent blue coloration on its forewings but is missing the hindwing stripes that give this species its common name.

Striped blue crow
Euploea mulciber

The striped blue crow belongs to an Indo-Australian genus called crow butterflies because of their dark purple, black, brown, or blue iridescence, which reminds observers of crows taking wing in sunlight. The striped blue is often singled out as the most handsome of the crows. Only the female has stripes—white lines on the hindwings—although both sexes have a strong blue sheen.

Adults are mimicked sex for sex by *Papilio paradoxa* and other unrelated butterfly species.

Ranging from India and southern China to Malaysia, the Philippines, and other islands in the Indian Ocean, the numerous subspecies of striped blue crow average 3½ to 4 inches (9 to 10 cm) in wingspan. Although typically sighted in clearings and beside roads, this butterfly is associated with tropical forests, where it flies through tracks and along rivers carved through the rain forest. Attracted to flowering trees and shrubs, striped blue crows seek out oleander, figs, milkweed, and various pipevines as larval host-plants, which pass along toxins to the caterpillars and make them unpalatable to predators.

Striped blue crows sometimes fly with other species of crows, and many roost communally. The males bask in the sun and are attracted to salty patches, dog and other mammal feces, urine, and mud. During courtship, male crows extend their abdominal hair pencils and release strongly scented pheromones that bystanders insist smell repulsive when the males appear in large numbers.

Caterpillars are yellowish brown, with pale or darker rings, and sport four pairs of long red filaments with black tips. The chrysalides of most crows, when discovered hanging from a fig tree, look like "shining artificial Christmas-tree baubles," says entomologist Robert Goodden, and their metallic gold or gold-green color is so shiny that an observer can actually see his or her reflection in it.

Striped blue crow chrysalis
The mirrorlike chrysalis of a striped blue crow has a metallic gold-green surface that reminds some observers of a gold Christmas tree ornament. Butterfly collectors were once called "Aurelians" after the golden reflections of chrysalids like these.

Zebra longwing

Heliconius charithonia

The zebra longwing looks quite unlike any other butterfly in the world. Instantly recognizable by its elongated black or chocolate-brown wings and prominent lemon-yellow zebra stripes, the zebra is unique not only physically but behaviorally as well.

While taxonomists wrangle over its proper scientific name (*Heliconius charithonia, charithonius, charitonius,* or *charitonia*) and common name (zebra heliconian is widely recognized), the zebra indisputably claims the title of state butterfly of Florida, where it resides year-round. It is also a resident of southern Texas, tropical and subtropical Central and South America, and the West Indies. (Vagrants are sometimes spotted in the Carolinas and as far west as Nebraska and California.) One of three North American butterflies called longwings due to their elongated fore- and hindwings, the zebra is also celebrated for its long lifespan—nine months, compared to the butterfly norm of only a few weeks. (Douglas calls zebra longwings "the Methuselahs of the butterfly world.")

Typically seen in tropical hammocks, scrub and open areas, and along woodland

Zebra longwing

An adult zebra longwing nectars on Buddha's belly. This unusually long-lived species extends its lifespan by collecting pollen, which it breaks down into protein with digestive enzymes and then absorbs through the proboscis.

and pine-forest borders, the zebra longwing seems to prefer disturbed and second-growth habitats to primary forests, and turns up in gardens bordered by woodland.

The dark ground color, so conspicuous on both sides of the wings, is interrupted by bold yellow stripes, with rosy spots underneath near the base of the hindwings. With a wingspan of 2¾ to 4 inches (7.2 to 10.2 cm), this butterfly has an unusually slow and deliberate flight, characterized by some observers as feeble or shivering and imparting a rather ghostly appearance. But no matter how slow or weak the wingbeats appear, they provide a speedy escape when predators approach.

At night, zebra longwings roost in flocks of up to seventy or more, congregating at the same favored site for many days until moving on. Zebras are characterized as unusually social creatures and are also judged to be some of the most intelligent butterflies; accordingly, scientists have developed several hypotheses to explain the communal roosting. The function of roosts may be to serve as "brokerage houses of information about the habitat," naturalist Allen Young suggests in *Sarapiquí Chronicle*. Newly emerged adults "might learn to locate pollen and nectar sources by following older, more experienced adult butterflies," he explains, and roosts "might also encourage the assembly of unmated, fresh females for mating."

Or, Young continues, females that have just mated "may learn to find caterpillar food plants on which to lay their eggs by following older, experienced females from the roost." Another explanation might be "a sort of collective defense against predators," he says, with members of the colony winging to safety when a

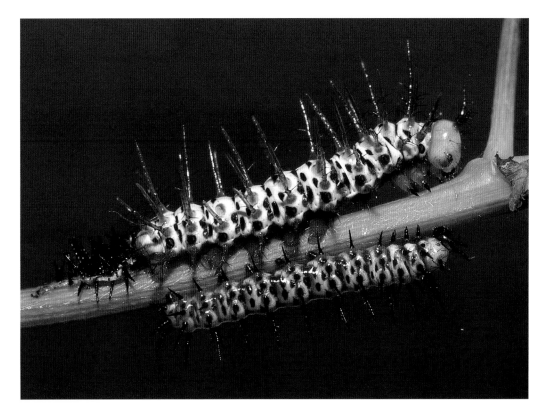

predator arrives or reinforcing their undesirability as prey via a "collective visual signal."

The reason zebra longwings are so unappetizing is their diet: the larvae dine on poisonous passionflower vines. Consequently, longwing caterpillars and adults are nauseating or even deadly if consumed. Adults sip nectar from a variety of flowers, especially white and blue varieties, but are unusual in also feeding on pollen. Since pollen is rich in protein, scientists credit it with extending the zebra's lifespan.

Another curious behavior is the adult male's attraction to female pupae. Males can detect the scent of a female, and Kenney reports many instances of seeing male zebra longwings resting on the female's chrysalis, waiting for her to emerge. According to Emmel,

Zebra longwing caterpillars
These two zebra longwing caterpillars are at different stages (instars) of growth between molts. The caterpillar above, in its third instar, has just shed its skin, separating it from the body with a digestive molting fluid; the caterpillar below, still in its second instar, is smaller.

Zebra longwings
Zebra longwings roost communally, hanging motionless in groups of up to seventy and returning nightly to the same site. This may be a defense against predators—safety in numbers—or a way to share information, following other individuals in the morning to nectar and pollen sources or to female pupae.

males sometimes fight one another for the opportunity to mate with a female once she has burst through her pupal skin. "This behavior has been called 'pupal rape,' since the female may be too weak immediately after emerging to effectively resist. 'Rape' may not be an accurate description, because the female may be consenting," he writes in *Florida's Fabulous Butterflies*. Some males do not wait, however, and instead "mate with her inside the chrysalis case." Afterward, the male transfers a chemical to the female that repels other suitors.

Adult females lay as many as one thousand eggs during their long lifespan, depositing conical golden-yellow ribbed eggs singly or in small clusters on buds or leaves of the toxic hostplants. The caterpillars are white or bluish white, with six rows of branched black spines and assorted black dots. The chrysalis "looks like it could be Hades' gate-keeper," Mikula declares, thanks to a ghoulish pair of antler-like projections on the head and numerous spines on the brownish-orange shell, which is adorned with silver or dark spots.

Gulf fritillary

Agraulis vanillae

The spectacular Gulf fritillary resembles many other members of the fritillary tribe, yet, curiously, it is the lone species in its genus and not even a true fritillary. True fritillaries are widespread but often difficult to differentiate (Scott counts some thirty species in North America, from the Arctic to Mexico). The wings of Gulf fritillaries, however, like those of their heliconian relatives, are longer and more slender than the rounded forewings of true fritillaries.

Fritillaries are named not for their onomatopoetic frittering or fluttering but for their resemblance to the red-orange flowers of fritillary plants. "Gulf" refers to the butterfly's frequent sightings near or over the waters of the Gulf of Mexico.

A fast flyer with shallow wingbeats, this butterfly has a wingspan of 2½ to 3 inches (6.0 to 7.5 cm). The uppersides are a rich orange or red orange, with prominent black veins and three white-centered dark spots on each forewing, and a broad dark border on the hindwings. The showy undersides are pale orange, orange brown, or tan, festooned with elongated silver spots that shimmer like mica. While pigmented scales create the orange hues, the iridescent silver markings are produced "when light is refracted through prisms in the wing scales," Emmel explains. This radiant silver gleam inspired the Comstocks to characterize the butterfly as "a bit of animated sunshine."

Gulf fritillaries range from the southern United States through Central America to

Argentina, but late-summer migrants may visit Michigan, Wisconsin, and the north-central states or fly west to California. In 1977, the species was introduced to Hawaii, where it has since become well-established.

Favored habitats include open meadows, brushy fields, woodland edges, utility easements, city parks, and suburban gardens. The chief enticement, at least for females, is the presence of passionflower vine—the hostplant for the larvae. The biological benefit is obvious: *Passiflora* are toxic, providing caterpillars (as well as adults) with a chemical defense. In fact, the Gulf fritillary seems to have "a total disregard for its own safety," says Patrick Hook, "because its predators have learned the hard way that it will make them very sick if they eat it." At night, Gulf fritillaries sometimes roost in clusters on grass or on low-growing woody plants near hostplants. Adults sip nectar from flowers and are particularly fond of lantana and butterfly bushes, as well as zinnias, asters, verbena, and Mexican sunflowers.

Gulf fritillaries

A pair of Gulf fritillaries roost on lantana. The spectacular undersides of their wings are adorned with iridescent silver spots that refract light through prisms in the wing scales. One large spot on each hindwing suggests a threatening eye and may startle predators.

two longer spines curving backward on the head. The chrysalis is usually mottled brown, gray brown, or greenish brown, with a reddish band on the abdomen, pink spots on the head, and black-and-silver markings.

Small postman
Heliconius erato

Co-mimics—that's what scientists call the small postman (or erato) and the postman (*Heliconius melpomene*), two of the most celebrated Müllerian mimics in lepidopteran literature. Some 125 years ago, explorer Fritz Müller argued that a close resemblance between two or more unpalatable species would benefit all, since predators might learn to shun all distasteful look-alikes after just one encounter. Of the many butterfly doppelgängers, these two heliconians are among the most intriguing, because each of the dozen or more distinct races of postman, common from Mexico to Brazil, has a nearly identical local race of small postman.

Gulf fritillary

A Gulf fritillary displays handsome orange red on the upperside of its wings, accented with dark spotting and veins, as it nectars on scarlet milkweed. The shiny orange and black caterpillars feed on passionflower leaves, ingesting toxins that make both the larval and adult forms distasteful to vertebrate predators.

"Their bold color patterns change dramatically, but always together, from region to region," Phil Schappert reports; "within any given part of their range, the two species look more alike than do the same species from two adjacent regions. There is almost perfect geographic concordance in the regionality of their patterns."

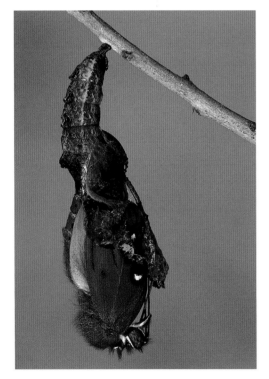

Gulf fritillary

A Gulf fritillary emerges from its mottled gray-brown chrysalis, resembling a dead leaf, after about twelve days. These year-round residents of Florida and regions bordering the Gulf of Mexico are late-season migrants farther north, emerging from chrysalides in Tennessee sometimes as late as November.

Males patrol in search of females and court by hovering above or landing beside a prospective mate and flapping their wings as many as thirty times in five seconds to waft pheromones to her antennae, Scott reports. The female lays yellow eggs singly on leaves, stems, or tendrils of hostplants, and hatchling caterpillars (extremely tiny at first, though they bulk up over successive molts and attain a rather breathtaking length) are decked out every bit as flamboyantly as their parents. The larvae sport two glossy orange-red stripes that run lengthwise on a gleaming black or bluish-black ground color; prominent adornments include six rows of sinister black spines and

The small postman and its slightly larger co-mimic derive their name from an apparent resemblance to nineteenth-century British postmen, who wore dark frock coats with scarlet collars, cuffs, and piping. Similarly hued, the small postman and postman are both

Small postman *(Heliconius erato petiverana)*
The small postman, or erato, is a highly variable Neotropical butterfly renowned for its diversity of regional subspecies and its classic Müllerian mimicking of the postman butterfly (*Heliconius melpomene*). The individual here represents the subspecies *H. erato petiverana*, which ranges from Mexico to Panama.

black with a bold red band (sometimes orange or yellow) across the forewing; other color and pattern variations include orange rays on the hindwings and a large white spot on each forewing tip. The wingspan of the small postman is 2¼ to 3¼ inches (5.5 to 8 cm).

This butterfly, which strays into southern Texas, roosts at night in small colonies, sometimes with other species, and returns repeatedly to the same location for weeks or even months. Favoring Neotropical forest margins, disturbed woodland habitats, open pastures, and coffee plantations, the small postman flies low to the ground, sometimes with its co-mimics, although this species shows a greater preference for direct sunlight. Males patrol in search of females, often nudging a prospective mate to fly and then fanning her with pheromones—which, when transferred to her stink clubs, produce an odor that de-

ters other males. Eager males also search for pupae and mate with emerging females.

Females lay their eggs singly on passion-flower vines, avoiding plants where they see another egg—perhaps because the caterpillars are "notoriously cannibalistic," Watson and Whalley report. But, for their part, passion-flower vines have evolved their own defenses against heliconians. Gilbert has found that some *Passiflora* deter ovipositing females by generating buds or spots that resemble eggs. He also identified a passionflower that kills caterpillars by hooking its hairs into the larvae, and discovered plants whose nectar glands attract predatory ants that feed on heliconian larvae.

Small postman caterpillars are white with black spots, a buff-colored head capsule, long black head spines, and shorter body spines. The chrysalis is light brown with spines and gold spots and reportedly makes soft sounds.

Small postman *(Heliconius erato cyrbia)*
This subspecies of small postman, *Heliconius erato cyrbia*, is from Ecuador. The iridescent blue is accentuated by characteristically bright red bands on the elongated forewings and white rays on the hindwings.

Small postman *(Heliconius erato erato)*
H. erato erato, one of many other regional subspecies of small postman (form andremona), is found in the Republic of Suriname in South America. The bright orange hindwing rays warn of the insect's unpalatability, due to larval consumption of poisonous passionflower foliage.

Small postman *(Heliconius erato notabilis)*
Another regional subspecies of small postman, Ecuador's *H. erato notabilis*, flaunts its arresting white bands, tinged with pale red, on contrasting dark wings.

It is not improbable that had there been no revolution in Russia, I would have devoted myself entirely to lepidopterology and never have written any novels at all.

—Vladimir Nabokov

Hecale
Heliconius hecale

One of the most common heliconian residents of Central America and northern South America, the hecale is known under a host of aliases, including brown longwing, common tiger longwing, hecale's longwing, golden helicon, and zuleika. This species varies highly in color and pattern: some individuals have dark wings with yellow spots and bands, while others have white or yellow spots with vivid red or reddish-orange bands. Several subspecies also have iridescent blue stripes on the underside. With so much variation, it's not surprising that the hecale's mimics belong to more than one genus of butterfly.

Found in all types of habitats, from rain forests to open pastures, these longwings have been observed by DeVries flying through Costa Rican mountain passes from Pacific to Atlantic slopes—leading him to hypothesize that the species is migratory. At night, hecales often roost in the forest subcanopy.

The hecale has a wingspan of about 1⅗ to 2 inches (4.2 to 5.0 cm) and is a slow flyer, although predators avoid these butterflies due to their unpalatability. Like most longwings, the hecale lays its eggs on poisonous passionflower vines, which confer a toxic defense on caterpillars as well as adults. Scientists believe the butterfly's bright red, orange, or yellow colors, starkly set off against a black background, are aposematic, advertising the insect's noxious taste. The caterpillar's bright chalky-white torso, contrasting bright orange head, and black spines and spots may serve as warning colors, too. The chrysalis is brown with gold spots and black spines.

Question mark

Polygonia interrogationis

The question mark, at one time known as the "interrogation butterfly," shares with its relatives the commas the curious distinction of being named after a punctuation mark.

"Interrogation point" was a once-fashionable synonym for "question mark," and clearly both popular labels were conceived for identification purposes—to call attention to a distinctive silver marking on the underside of the hindwing. Some observers, however, insist

Question mark

The question mark butterfly, named for the small but distinctive silver punctuation mark on the underside of its hindwing, rests in leaf litter on the forest floor. When it folds its orange wings over its body, the muted browns of the underside and the ragged outline of its anglewings help this species blend into its surroundings.

Question mark

A question mark butterfly emerges from a well-camouflaged chrysalis that masquerades as a dead leaf. This species is unusually active during the chrysalid stage, swinging forcefully back and forth when disturbed.

that this bright crescent marking with a dot actually looks more like a semicolon, so an alternative explanation is offered: Johann Fabricius, the European collector who first described and named the species *interrogationis*, may have likened the shape of the chrysalis to an interrogation mark.

Whatever his logic, the grammar label stuck—and today this striking butterfly is of interest for other characteristics as well.

As a member of the anglewing clan, the question mark is distinguished by the ragged outline of its wings—highly effective camouflage that replicates a weathered leaf. The coloration of this species is noteworthy, too, since this butterfly is seasonally dimorphic: the summer form has dark hindwings, and the winter form has orange. In fact, the two forms differ so markedly that they were once believed to be different species. The brighter upperside is mottled orange and brown, with dark spotting and dark highlights around the edges. The underside is lighter ("a gentle mosaic of subtle browns and orange," says Mikula), with a lavender tinge on the outer margins of the wings and tails and an iridescent gleam. As soon as the butterfly lands, it closes its showy wings, shifting abruptly to the underside's cryptic coloration that resembles a dead leaf. The wingspan averages 2¼ to 3 inches (5.8 to 7.6 cm).

Question marks range from southern Canada across the United States east of the Rocky Mountains to southern Arizona and central Mexico. They are common in wooded areas, forest edges, sunny clearings, streamsides, fencerows, parks, suburban yards, and, when migrating, dunes and beaches. Unlike most butterflies, adults prefer rotting fruit, tree sap, carrion, and dung to nectar—and, if the fruit has fermented, the question mark has a "habit of getting drunk," Emmel discloses.

In the afternoon, males set up territories, perching on tree trunks and waiting to be approached by prospective mates. Females lay long, pale-green eggs singly or in pairs—or piled on top of one another in loose clusters—on elm, nettle, false nettle, hackberry, basswood, or hops. The caterpillars are black or rusty brown with irregular silver spots, and orange or yellow lateral stripes on each side. Orange branching spines appear in rows on the body, and the head sports a pair of black branching spines. The gray-brown chrysalis has gold or silver spots, dorsal cones, and two short horns; it is unusually active and, if disturbed, will swing rapidly back and forth. In the early 1900s, the chrysalides were called "hop merchants," Dickerson recalls. "If they show a large amount of gold coloring, hops are to sell high, so say the hop-growers; if there is more silver than gold, hops will be low."

In late fall, adults engage in spectacular migrations, flying south along the Atlantic coastline. Some adults overwinter in the northern United States, however, often inside hollow trees, and on a warm day a few hibernators may emerge, says Klots, "presenting the spectacle of butterflies flying over the snow."

Painted lady

Vanessa cardui

During the Victorian era, London streetwalkers who applied rouge and lipstick to their faces were called "painted ladies"—a label that soon reached the American West, where miners applied it to saloon "hostesses" who favored similar makeup. And thus, "after a hard day of working the claims, a Forty-Niner's thoughts would turn to his favorite lady," Makula explains. "The wash of pink on the underwing of the painted lady reminded him of his favorite lady."

Such an explanation sounds plausible, since this migratory enchantress is daubed with orange, brown, and white, with hints of pale rose and purple, and garnished with black diamonds and spots. Not to be confused

Painted lady
A painted lady spreads its wings while nectaring on lantana. The white spots visible on the upperside of its forewings appear only against the dark brown tip, whereas the similar American painted lady (*Vanessa virginiensis*) also has two small white spots on an orange background.

111

Painted lady

A row of small eyespots adorns the intricate wing pattern on the underside of a painted lady, which is known for its great migrations between North Africa and Europe. The red admiral is often a companion on these migratory flights.

with her three "lady" friends—the American lady (*Vanessa virginiensis*), West Coast lady (*V. annabella*), and red admiral (*V. atalanta*)—the painted lady is found the world over and said to be the most widely distributed butterfly on the planet.

Spreading her wings 2 to 2⅞ inches (5.0 to 7.3 cm), the painted lady has four small eyespots on the underside of each hindwing, which help to distinguish the species from the American lady's two larger eyespots. The cryptically colored underside has ornate patterns of mottled brown and white, with a rosy or purple tint, which observers have likened to a cobweb woven by a Persian loom.

The painted lady's habitats are as diverse as her range: Scott says the species' habitat is "everywhere"—especially open and disturbed areas. Fields, dunes, gardens, and marshes are favored sites, but deserts, Pacific islands, and Alpine meadows provide temporary stops during migration. Adults overwinter but perish if exposed to freezing temperatures, so painted ladies take wing in giant swarms, some migrating from Mexico to the United States and Canada in the spring, then back again in the fall. On occasion, these masses have been truly memorable: in 1924, for example, a swarm passing through the American Southwest en route to California was reportedly 40 miles (64 km) wide. The size of such flocks varies from year to year, however, and end-of-the-season return flights are generally smaller. Major migrations take place in Europe, too, and large swarms cross the Mediterranean every spring from Africa.

Its worldwide presence has earned this butterfly the names "cosmopolitan" and "cosmopolite," but its botanical craving accounts for the more universal name "thistle butterfly." Adults conspicuously seek out thistles for nectar, but they reportedly feed on more than one hundred other plants. Eggs, normally pale green, are laid singly on the leaf tips of hostplants. Caterpillars live individually in silk nests, weaving hostplant leaves together with pieces of thistle and other plant fibers. The caterpillars vary in color, from black or grayish brown with white speckles to dull or yellow green. Yellow stripes run down the sides, hairy yellow or orange bristles dot the back, and the underside is rusty brown. The chrysalis is green, bluish white, or cream-colored, with gold points and dark patches; to the untrained eye, it looks like a dried-up leaf.

Malachite

Siproeta stelenes

A green mineral called malachite has given its name to a butterfly of the same color—a creature Ken Preston-Mafham calls "one of the most beautiful of all the world's green butterflies." This large butterfly is widespread throughout Central and South America, but populations now thrive in southern Florida and extreme southern Texas and are expanding their range. (A solitary stray once showed up in Kansas.)

Imagine a swallowtail inexplicably tinted emerald, and you have some idea what this butterfly looks like. Its prominent translucent green patches and spots, set against a brown-black background, command attention immediately; its gray or light-brown underside has pale green markings and

Malachite
The spectacular malachite butterfly, named after a bright-green mineral, established itself in Florida in the 1960s after straying north from the West Indies and Mexico. This individual prepares to nectar on a red passionflower.

Malachite
Translucent emerald-green markings on the malachite's brownish-black wings make this species one of the world's most gorgeous green butterflies. Known for its graceful aerial gliding, the malachite—shown resting here on a banana leaf—sips juices from rotting fruit as well as from flowers.

red-orange lines. But the butterfly's stunning green hues begin to fade within days of its emergence, and older adults are less dramatically colored.

The malachite has a large wingspan of 3¼ to 4 inches (8.1 to 10.2 cm) and short hindwing tails, which enhance its distinctiveness when it floats by in its characteristically slow and lazy manner, often just a few feet above the ground. Its habitats include tropical hammocks, subtropical forests, forest edges, shady paths, clearings, wooded ravines, and overgrown citrus groves, but malachites also visit gardens and open areas near woods in search of rotting fruit, dung, carrion, and nectar. At night, adults roost in small groups on low-growing shrubs; by day, individuals commonly rest with their wings open on large-leaf plants such as bananas.

Males perch or patrol in search of mates. Females lay dark-green eggs singly or in clusters of two or three on the underside of unfolding leaves of green shrimp plants, ruellia, acanthus, cafetin, and plantago. Mature caterpillars, which grow to 2 inches (5.1 cm), are velvety black with dark-red or purple divisions between segments. Dorsal spines, rising from orange spots, are red or reddish yellow; two long-branched horns on the head are red or black. The spines may trigger an allergic rash if they touch human skin; in addition, researchers report, larvae sometimes "spit" a greenish fluid when disturbed. Chrysalides, mainly green with black spots, have rows of pink spikes on the abdomen and two dark horns on the head.

Ruddy daggerwing

Marpesia petreus

The ruddy daggerwing would appear well-equipped for a duel: it brandishes a pair of long brown tails on its hindwings—more swordlike than daggerlike, actually—which, together with hook-shaped forewings, present a decidedly distinctive appearance. The upperside of the wings is ruddy orange or orange brown, crossed by three parallel dark lines, while the underside is paler, mottled with pinkish brown; this cryptic dead-leaf color likely provides a degree of protection. Near each swordlike tail is a "false head" that may draw a predator's attention away from the more vulnerable real head.

The ruddy daggerwing is found in tropical Central and South America south to Brazil, but also occurs in southern Florida and Texas and sometimes strays north to Colorado, Nebraska, and Kansas. Its favored habitat is hardwood hammocks—especially those with fig trees—as well as subtropical woodland areas, evergreen forests, and open swampy locales. The fig offers a dual enticement: hungry caterpillars devour the leaves of the strangler fig, short-leaved fig, banyan, and other figs (as well as mulberry and cashews), and the overripe fruit attracts adults. Females lay small pale-yellow or white eggs singly on hostplant leaves. The vividly colored caterpillars are purple, bright orange, or reddish brown, with wide yellow saddles on the back and black dashes on the side; they also sport a row of four dark spines down the back and a pair of long recurved horns on the head. The chrysalis is light green or grayish white

Ruddy daggerwing
The dramatic coloration of the ruddy daggerwing suggests a holiday carnival: bright tropical orange laced with thin tiger stripes, embellished with a pair of stiletto-like tails. Males perch high in sunlit trees to watch for females but will descend to investigate any bright orange object that catches their eye.

with black speckling, long black spines, and, on the head, curved black-and-green spines.

Adults have a wingspan of 2¾ to 3¾ inches (7.0 to 9.5 cm) and are exceptionally swift and agile. They often fly high above fig trees in full sun, sometimes in the company of julias, descending to nectar on flowers, sip juice from rotting fruit, or gather at riverbanks to mud-puddle. Territorial males will fly down to inspect bright orange objects, so to attract a ruddy daggerwing, Glassberg suggests tossing an orange into the air or waving orange fabric.

Shoemaker

Archaeoprepona demophon

Numerous problems exist with the nomenclature of the genus *Archaeoprepona*, and some taxonomists classify butterflies from this group in the genus *Prepona*. Although little is known of their life history, this much is apparent: species belonging to this genus are very rapid fliers, and some entomologists believe they are the fastest butterflies in the world.

Shoemaker
Some researchers believe that the shoemaker, a mango-loving forest inhabitant of the Neotropics, may be the fastest flier in the butterfly world.

A resident of Central America and the islands of Cuba, Hispaniola, and Puerto Rico south to the Amazon Basin, *Archaeoprepona demophon* has more than one common name—shoemaker, king shoemaker, banded king shoemaker, and one-spotted prepona—creating confusion with another "shoemaker" (*Catonephele antinoe*) of an altogether different species. How these butterflies came to be known as shoemakers is unclear, although one author supposes the name derives from the fairy tale "The Shoemaker and the Elves," since butterflies were once thought to be fairies or winged elves. Or perhaps the name refers to the similarity of the wings to wooden forms used to make shoes.

This strikingly handsome butterfly has a large metallic-blue or blue-green band on the dark upperside of each wing, with iridescence like that of a black-velvet painting. On the underside, the coloration is tan or pale gray, with dark brown on the inner margins of the forewings. The wingspan is 4 to 4¾ inches (10 to 12 cm). Observers say these butterflies make a rustling or crackling sound when in flight ("like thick paper being screwed up," note Watson and Whalley), audible from a distance of several meters.

Entomologist Albert Schwartz recalls strolling down a stretch of road on Hispaniola, wearing a pale blue hat, when a shoemaker twice landed on his hat, apparently attracted to the blue. In Costa Rica, males have been observed chasing rival butterflies. Individuals race in "long erratic circles around a large tree," DeVries says, after which they return to their perches on tree trunks, heads pointed downward. Shoemakers are found in hardwood forests, clearings, and on avocado plantations, and are glimpsed patrolling ravines and pathways. Reportedly these butterflies sometimes smell like vanilla.

Shoemakers are attracted to rotting fruits, especially mangoes, and apparently do not nectar on flowers. Females lay round white eggs singly on soursop trees and other hostplants. Caterpillars are brown with dark tails, yellow spots, and a pair of short horns on the head. The chrysalis is blue green with light spots that resemble lichen.

Indian leaf butterfly

Kallima inachus

Masquerading as a dry or dying leaf, the Indian leaf butterfly has been vexing naturalists and collectors for more than two centuries. A classic example of cryptic coloration, this species exhibits what some experts consider the finest camouflage of any butterfly in the world.

Ranging from India and Pakistan eastward to China and Taiwan, the Indian leaf is one of about ten species of *Kallima*—of which, curiously, no two individuals of any species look exactly alike, D'Abrera says. Taxonomists have wrangled over the nomenclature for years, he adds, and "the many seasonal forms have all been bestowed names *ad nauseam*." The familiar names leaf, oak leaf, or dead-leaf butterfly derive from the uncommon shape of the wing. But the secret to this insect's success is even more complex: its profile, coloration, markings, and strategically placed tails conspire to hoodwink humans and predators alike.

Indian leaf butterfly
At first glance, the bright upperside of an Indian leaf butterfly's wings would appear to account for the species' gift for evading predators. If disturbed, the butterfly may expose its flash colors, startling the intruder and gaining time for a quick getaway.

Indian leaf butterfly

The Indian leaf butterfly's reputation as a master illusionist is in fact based on cryptic coloration, pattern, and wing shape. When the wings are folded, the butterfly's drab brown underside instantly mimics a dead leaf, complete with veinlike dark lines, mold- or funguslike spots, and wing tails that resemble stems.

The first deception is the distinctive point on each forewing, which mimics the tip of a leaf. When the butterfly folds its wings, they create the profile of a leaf. The illusion is complete, because the tail on the hindwing resembles a stem. This reconfigured silhouette would offer little protection if the bright orange and purplish blue on the upperside remained visible, but now only the drab dead-leaf coloration on the underside is displayed. A conspicuous false mid-rib runs down the center, and dark stripes resemble veins. Other markings replicate leaf mold, fungus, plant decay, and leaf tears.

No wonder the English naturalist Alfred Russel Wallace complained that he "often endeavoured to capture it without success, for after flying a short distance, it would enter a bush among dry or dead leaves...In its position of repose it so closely resembled a dead leaf attached to a twig as almost certainly to deceive the eye when gazing fully on it." To minimize its shadow, it tilts its body vis-à-vis the sun.

The Indian leaf butterfly's wingspan is 3½ to 5 inches (8.9 to 12.7 cm). "When pursued by a predator (or excited scientist)," Hook writes, the butterfly "flies at great speed and then stops dead." Rarely seen in the open, this species favors tropical forests with heavy rainfall, woodsy undergrowth, valleys, and riverbanks. Adults are attracted to rotting fruit, particularly bananas, and to tree sap. The velvety black caterpillars, bearing red spines and long yellowish hairs, feed on *Girardinia*, *Strobilanthus*, acanthus, and polygonum herbs.

Although members of the genus are not native to North America, the species *Kallima paraletka* has been adopted as the logo for the Rocky Mountain Butterfly Consortium, having inspired one of the original founders of the Butterfly Pavilion and Insect Center in Westminster, Colorado.

Variable cracker

Hamadryas feronia

It sounds like an odd name for a butterfly, but the variable cracker warrants it. Males fly directly at each other, apparently to defend a territory or confront a rival, and make an audible cracking, crackling, or clicking noise while in flight. Other crackers, all members of the genus *Hamadryas*, make these sounds too, perhaps using spiny rods on the tip of the abdomen or wing-tip veins, although scientists aren't satisfied that they know the true purpose.

Native to Central and South America as far south as Brazil and Paraguay, the variable (or blue) cracker regularly strays into the lower Rio Grande Valley of southern Texas. It occurs in forest habitats, including tropical rain forests, and is often seen on the margins of wooded areas and in open areas. Crackers are also called calico butterflies because of the intense blotching of spots and patches on their wings. This particular cracker has pale blue or bluish gray rings around eyespots—black with white centers—on the upperside of the hindwing and a red bar on the forewing. The underside is lighter, with tan or yellowish patches and black rings on the hindwing. The wingspan is 2⅛ to 3¼ inches (5.3 to 8.2 cm).

Crackers characteristically perch on tree trunks with their wings outstretched and head pointed downward. "Lean against a shade tree at the edge of a clearing," says Cassie, "and one or more crackers may magically appear from the tree bark, where they have been resting in their camouflage garb." In Costa Rica, crackers may exhibit vertical stratifica-tion in some habitats: like anole lizards and other animals, different species may occupy discrete zones or levels of the forest canopy. Prior to sunset, adults congregate at one tree, then disperse to roost under nearby leaves.

Adult crackers do not visit flowers, feeding instead on rotting fruit and animal dung. Favored hostplants for larvae are tropical vines in the spurge family. Eggs are laid singly or in chains, and some caterpillars engage in gregarious behavior, sharing their hostplants. Variable cracker caterpillars are black (or blue black) with whitish dots and red spots, or sometimes a dirty grayish green with a pale stripe; yellow spines on the body resemble those of a bottlebrush. On its head, the chrysalis sports two long, flattened horns.

> *Literature and butterflies are the two sweetest passions known to man.*
>
> —Vladimir Nabokov

Variable cracker
The variable cracker typically positions itself head down on a tree trunk as it awaits the arrival of a prospective mate. Male crackers produce an audible "clicking" noise in flight, apparently to challenge an intruder or rival or to defend a territory.

Mexican sister or Admiral adelpha

Adelpha fessonia

Sisters are precious, and keeping their names straight is understandably important. Among the sisterhood of *Adelpha*, however, confusion is unavoidable. For example, *A. fessonia* (formerly *Limenitis fessonia*) is known variously as the Mexican sister, band-celled sister, or admiral adelpha; moreover, this *Adelpha* is not always easy to distinguish from the other 250 named forms and races.

"The butterflies that compose the genus *Adelpha* are, in my opinion, the most difficult and trying taxonomically of all the nymphalids," DeVries declares. The adults look remarkably similar, few life histories have been described, "and the nomenclature is chaotic," he concludes.

The sisters are Neotropical butterflies, distributed throughout Central and South America. The Mexican sister is found from central Mexico south to Panama, but it regularly strays into the lower Rio Grande Valley of Texas. The sisters all have brown uppersides with an orange patch on the forewing tip, but this species can be identified by a prominent white band that runs across the forewing and hindwing. The wingspan of this butterfly is 2³⁄₁₆ to 2¾ inches (5.6 to 7.0 cm).

Mexican sister
The Mexican sister, or admiral adelpha, is a native of Central America and a periodic visitor to the lower Rio Grande Valley, where it is known as the band-celled sister. Prominent white bands, accompanied by orange tips on the forewings, distinguish this member of the flap-and-glide family of sisters.

Clipper
More than thirty geographical color morphs, races, or subspecies of clipper butterflies are currently recognized. The characteristic dark striped pattern is the same, but the base color on the upperwings varies dramatically from location to location.

This particular sister is rare in rain forests but fairly common in lowland and deciduous forests where there is a recurrent dry season; it prefers edges of forests and streamside trails. Adults nectar on flowers of croton and *Cordia*, but also feed on rotting fruit on the ground and in the forest canopy. One North American relative, the California sister (*Adelpha bredowii*), is said to be attracted to sweet grape juice spilled at vineyards.

Females lay their eggs singly on host-plants that include hackberry and *Randia*; the larvae are spiny and apparently do not rely on cryptic coloration for protection. "None of the species hides under cover," DeVries states; "all sit on top of leaves or in exposed places." The larvae of all species make frass chains, and many create exclusive resting areas on the surface of leaves. The chrysalis is brown or green or has a reflective chromelike color. When a male butterfly emerges, it often heads for mud or damp sand. Adult *Adelpha* males regularly perch on the edge of a forest or high in the canopy, moving repeatedly and chasing away other insect intruders.

Clipper

Parthenos sylvia

The clipper is a magnificent butterfly of innumerable subspecies that has a powerful effect on many who glimpse it for the first time. "In flight, the species is a grand sight; it can be truly described as aristocratic or noble," D'Abrera writes. "Its effortless sailing with wings held dead flat makes one gasp in awe. I have seen experienced collectors…merely stand and stare, hypnotised….I suppose the expressions on their faces can best be described in American parlance [as] a 'double-take.'"

Exhibiting remarkable variability in pattern and color, the clipper is among the most photographed species in North American butterfly conservatories. (Its willingness to perch photogenically with wings outspread may be a factor.) Found from India across Malaysia to the Philippines and Papua New Guinea, this butterfly is likely to be green or blue green in western populations and greenish yellow or greenish brown in eastern populations. Translucent white patches contrast sharply with a mix of dark-brown patches, bands, and borders on the wings; orange-and-black stripes adorn the abdomen. The pattern on the underside of the wings is paler.

With a wingspan of 4 to 4¼ inches (10 to 10.8 cm), the clipper is a strong flier that soars high over trees in tropical forests and lower over scrub areas and clearings at the edge of forests. Clippers often bask in the sun for extended periods and mass in large numbers beside streams to drink. They are commonly sighted near villages, searching for lantana and other flowers on which to nectar. Females deposit eggs on passionflower vines and *Tinospora*. The caterpillars are green or yellow brown and sport dark-purple spines.

Clipper

The noble clipper of Malaysia often soars high over the tops of trees with its wings spread wide, exhibiting its distinctive but variable blue or green markings on a dark background.

Malay lacewing

Cethosia hypsea

The lacewings of Asia are an aptly named lot, as the undersides of their scalloped wings are trimmed with intricate patterns that resemble the edging on lace. One of the most striking examples is the Malay lacewing, a butterfly found throughout Malaysia and Myanmar to the Sunda Islands. The upperside of the wings is bright orange red, with prominent black borders on the serrated hindwing edges. The underside is even more vivid, with an intense orange-red patch above a creamy white mark adjacent to a light-orange band, highlighted with rows of spotted dark edging. Freshly emerged adult males have a rosy bloom over the main orange area. The outer wing borders are embroidered with arresting zigzags of white, stitched onto a black background. A second pattern, the so-called Jawi

Malay lacewing
The intricate patterns and attractive colors on the underside of a Malay lacewing are truly spectacular, with decorative wing borders reminiscent of delicate lacework.

(a form of Malay writing), appears just after the intricate lace pattern.

The Malay lacewing has a wingspan of 1⅗ to 1¾ inches (4.2 to 4.5 cm) and commonly flies along roadsides and around flowering prickly lantana and snakeweed (*Stachytarpheta indica*). Eggs are laid in small batches on passionflower vines—each egg "carefully deposited a measured distance from the next, like pins in a bowling alley,"

says Goodden. The toxic hostplants provide the gregarious caterpillars with a chemical defense against predators, and the caterpillar's aposematic color (wine red, with long spines) signals a warning. Adults sometimes exude an unpleasant odor when handled. At night, adult Malay lacewings roost communally.

Malay lacewing
Topside, the colors and patterns on the wings of a Malay lacewing suggest an altogether different species. The wings reveal a pronounced scalloping or serration, especially the hindwings.

Coolies
Coolie butterflies are a familiar sight on the island of Trinidad and throughout tropical South America, where they are known for their sun-worshipping. Coolies are easily identified by their deep scarlet and black wings with rows of white spots.

Coolie

Anartia amathea

The coolie is a strikingly handsome butterfly of Central and tropical South America, widespread and common from Panama to Argentina and on the islands of Trinidad and Tobago. Cassie calls the coolie "a slave to sunshine" and writes: "A field swarming with them one minute will appear barren the next if a large cloud obscures the sun." This species commonly basks alongside paths in gardens and cultivated areas and is also partial to roadsides and other man-made clearings. Undisturbed rain forests, on the other hand, are avoided, except along rivers.

The coolie, also called the red peacock, has a wingspan of 1½ to 2⅜ inches (3.8 to 5.9 cm), and its flight is characterized as swift and jaunty but erratic. The male flaunts broad red bands (pinkish in females) down the middle of the fore- and hindwings. Large areas of the outer margins are dark—generally black in males and brownish gray in females—with bands of white spots. The underside is tan, replicating the upperside's markings but lighter in color.

The hypothesis that coloration in species correlates with visual discrimination by the sexes in courtship has been tested experimentally with this species, and researchers have made two discoveries. Female coolies whose red bands were changed to black were considerably less attractive to males than conventional females, according to the Preston-Mafhams, yet females accepted males colored black all over as readily as they did normal-colored red-banded males. In this case, it is likely that sexual attractants are not exclusively visual.

Female coolies lay yellowish-green eggs on hostplants such as acanthus and verbena. Caterpillars are black with red branching spines, pale lateral stripes, and, on the head, long clubbed spines. The translucent chrysalis is jade green with dark spots or, on occasion, entirely black.

Giant charaxes

Charaxes castor

The giant charaxes, or giant castor, is a robust, brightly colored species abundant in the forests of southern Africa from Senegal to Kenya and Tanzania. The sexes look alike, both having a black or dark-blue upperside

Giant charaxes
The high-flying giant charaxes of southern Africa is a confrontational species that jostles other butterflies at feeding grounds with its strong forewings, notable for miniscule "teeth" along the forward edge.

with a pale-yellow band on each wing. The underside, however, is almost beyond description: a dramatic display of white zigzags, round or square outlines on dark brown or black, and long stretches of orange tan on the forewings, reddish brown on the hindwings, with blue along the edges. The average wingspan is a whopping 4⅜ inches (11 cm); females are larger than males and have long, curved tails.

Giant charaxes have strong wings and fly high and fast, according to tropical butterfly expert D. F. Owen. Their behavior has been characterized as pugnacious, especially when adults "joust" over their feeding grounds. Their powerful wings, when jerked rapidly, can be used as a weapon, sometimes inflicting damage on an opponent. "Frequently a larger *Charaxes* will displace a small individual and take its place at the food source," Owen writes. "The behaviour of *Charaxes* at rotten fruit is reminiscent of birds at a feeding table in winter; individual distances are maintained by aggressive postures."

Adults rarely visit flowers, preferring rotting fruit (especially bananas), oozing tree sap, decaying animal remains, and excrement. When sipping the juices of rotting fruit, *Charaxes* butterflies often overindulge; collectors have captured specimens with abdomens "so distended that, with incautious handling, the abdomen breaks and the fruit juice floods out," Owen notes. "This might be necessary refueling," he adds, "in view of their extremely powerful and sustained flight." Where plentiful food sources are found, these butterflies congregate in large numbers.

Males engage in hilltopping behavior in search of females, which lay their eggs on beans and other legumes. Caterpillars are green, dotted with black-and-white speckles, and have reddish eyespots and red horns; their head is smooth and hard, the remainder of the body rough.

Common morpho
Morpho peleides

At an altitude of two thousand feet, naturalist Archie Carr once glanced outside the window of a DC-3 and noticed "intermittent flashes of brilliant light, coming apparently from somewhere above the treetops." The tiny bursts of fire were all bright blue—huge morphos, it turned out, "flitting about, in and above the top forest level and changing the sun to hot turquoise on the metallic surfaces of their wings. I marveled that the small area of a butterfly wing could throw back to our height light so intense and so strong in color." The pilot, unimpressed, remarked that he had once witnessed the same spectacle at eight thousand feet.

Today, blue morphos are virtual icons of the Neotropics for environmentalists and tourists and count among the world's most spectacular butterflies. Heralded as "sentinels of sunshine" and "jewels of the jungle," morphos comprise some eighty species—and *Morpho peleides* is one of the most common. "Alive or dead, these insects demand attention," DeVries declares. Males are a brilliant iridescent blue on the upperside (females are somewhat less colorful), their underside a

dark chocolate brown patterned with large black- and yellow-rimmed eyespots.

Ranging from Mexico to Colombia and Venezuela, the common morpho inhabits rain forest canopies, forested and hilly areas, and coffee plantations, favoring established flyways such as forest corridors, trails, and streams. While hiking on a partly shaded forest trail in Brazil, Alexander and Elsie Klots caught sight of their first morpho and marveled: "Each time the butterfly passed through a shaft of sunlight, the flash of blue from the wings was like an unbelievably brilliant spark."

Yet whenever the morpho passed directly overhead, "we could suddenly see nothing but its dark, cryptically colored underside."

All this "flash and dazzle," naturalist Allen Young explains, is a highly effective defense strategy. "The dazzling colors of some species, coupled with a confusing pattern of flight involving lots of bobbing up and down, help to foil predators," he says. The earth tones on the underside permit the morpho to vanish against the forest backdrop "just for a split second, but long enough perhaps to confuse a bird on the wing as to

Common morpho
The brilliant blue iridescence of the common morpho, possibly the most famous butterfly of the Neotropics, has been glimpsed by pilots flying above the rain forest canopy at altitudes of up to eight thousand feet.

131

its exact location in flight." The effect, he concludes, is greatest among iridescent species, where the "contrast between conspicuousness and camouflage...is greatly enhanced." Curiously, the blue hues are created not by pigments but by refraction of light. Microscopic ridges and grooves on the wing's tiny scales, which are arranged in layered rows, refract rays of light and reflect only blue and ultraviolet wavelengths; due to variations in scale structure, every species has a "subtly different hue," authority Keith Porter notes.

The wingspan of the common morpho, 3¼ to 4¼ inches (9.5 to 12 cm), seems modest compared to that of certain other species: Cramer's blue morpho (*Morpho rhetenor*), for example, is 5 to 6 inches (13 to 15 cm), and others reach an astonishing 10 inches (26 cm). Bystanders routinely characterize their flight as zigzag, lazy, languid, or floppy. Males of this species typically patrol in the morning, while females are active only at midday. Adults feed on rotting fruit, fungi, and carrion.

Female common morphos lay dome-shaped eggs on plants in the pea family, including a wide assortment of legume vines and trees. The caterpillar has a hairy, mottled yellow-and-red body, two short tails, and a brownish red head with dense hairs. According to authority Dan Janzen, these hairs cause welts or itching when touched, and some observers report that the larvae emit a stench reminiscent of rancid butter.

Common morpho

A common morpho, already refracting intense light from the scales of its fresh wings, emerges through a split in its pale-green chrysalis.

Common morphos
During mating, common morphos raise their wings upright, revealing prominent black- and yellow-ringed eyespots on the underside. Airborne, the morpho flies in a characteristic zigzag, rather floppy fashion, readily recognized by viewers below.

Caterpillars feed for only about fifteen minutes at dawn and at dusk, according to Young, and are inactive for most of the remainder of the twenty-four-hour cycle. The chrysalis is pale green with a few shiny gold spots.

The majesty of the morpho has made this butterfly a prized trophy for collectors. Specimens routinely appear for sale on the Internet, mounted and framed for display, and commercial outfits use the wings in jewelry, lampshades, and other objects. Habitat destruction is primarily responsible for a decline in the relative number of morpho breeding populations. "It used to be a backyard species," says a founder of The Butterfly Farm in Costa Rica; "now it is found only in reserves."

Owl butterfly

Caligo eurilochus

The owl butterflies of Central and South America have tantalized collectors for years because of their uncanny resemblance—when their wings are spread and hindwing undersides are displayed upside down—to the face of an owl. In this pose, two enormous eyespots and a beak-shaped thorax create an elegant mimicry of an ominous raptor, which some scientists believe is a useful defense against predators.

But there's a catch: these eyespots are often hard to see when the butterfly is in flight, because *Caligo* flies erratically. Furthermore, owl butterflies are active at dawn and dusk, and their eyespots are difficult to distinguish in limited light. During the day, when this cryptically colored butterfly rests on a tree trunk, the two eyespots are never visible at the same time. And finally, for a predator to be fooled, it must associate the "owl face" with that of a previously encountered bird.

Owl butterflies

An owl butterfly displays one of its two large eyespots when it closes its wings. Scientists once believed these false eyes, viewed upside down alongside the beaklike body, mimicked the face of an owl. More likely, they mimic tree frog or lizard eyes, startling predators or diverting a bird attack toward an expendable wing edge.

For these reasons, scientists now tend to discount the owl-mimic hypothesis, but they do see other advantages to the markings. When an owl butterfly suddenly flaps its wings, the flash of its large eyespot may startle a predator, allowing the butterfly time to escape. Moreover, researchers have found evidence of beak damage directed toward the eyespots on *Caligo* wings, which suggests that the spots redirect a bird's attack away from more sensitive body parts. Researcher D. J. Stradling has proposed an alternative hypothesis: a raised hindwing with its prominent eyespot suggests the profile of a tree frog—which is not only distasteful but also sizeable enough to alarm an anole lizard or other predator.

Of the many species of owl butterflies, *Caligo eurilochus* is among the largest, with a wingspan that can reach 7⅛ inches (18.2 cm). This species has a gray-blue base on the upperside of the wings, with dark margins. The underside has intricate featherlike patterns and a large tan-ringed eyespot on each hindwing, along with several smaller spots. The underwings have a grayish wash.

Ranging from Guatemala to the Amazon Basin, this species is commonly found "in association with wet forest habitats," DeVries reports. It lives in agricultural areas, where it feeds on rotting fruit, especially overripe bananas. At dusk, owl butterflies "flit like brooding phantoms in the half light of the Brazilian jungles," observes Howe, and, due to their large size, are easily mistaken for bats.

Courtship chases are common among owl butterflies. Adults are remarkably agile, and their wings make a distinct sound, "described by some as a clatter," report John and

Maureen Tampion, but to them it sounds more like the "swish of soft velvet." The male brushes tufts of stiffened hairs against pheromone-producing pouches on each side of his abdomen, picking up the scent and transferring it to his wings, where the perfume evaporates into the heavy air, Young says. The male and female fly back and forth within a limited area, ensuring exposure to the airborne scents.

After mating, the female lays her eggs in small batches on banana plants, *Heliconia*, ginger lilies, cannas, and other plants. The caterpillars are gregarious, often lining up along a corridor of silky threads on the underside of a leaf. Originally green, the larvae turn brown after several molts; they sport prominent horns on the head capsule and have a forked tail. Caterpillars eat at night and sometimes wander away from their hostplant before developing into a chrysalis.

Owl butterfly caterpillar
This formal portrait of an owl butterfly caterpillar displays its fine brown-and-black masklike head, equipped with horns, hairs, cleavage lines, mandibles, and more.

Guatemalan satyr
The Guatemalan satyr has distinctive white bands on the underside that traverse the fore- and hindwings. Like many other satyrs, this species appears to "hop" when flying because of its slow wingbeats.

Guatemalan satyr

Cissia hesione

The Guatemalan, or hesione, satyr is a small brown butterfly distinguished by white bands on the underside of its wings. More than two thousand species of satyrs—named after the hairy, fun-loving half-human beasts of Greek mythology—populate the world, and members of this particular genus have created taxonomic quandaries for years. The genus *Cissia* ranges from the southern United States through Mexico to the Amazon Basin, according to DeVries, where the greatest species diversity has been recorded; the Guatemalan satyr ranges more narrowly from Mexico to Ecuador.

Satyr larvae feed on grasses or sedges, which accounts for the cryptic green or brown coloration of larvae and pupae. Scott believes the hearing organs of satyrs "may allow them to detect predators better," and he says that, in flight, the slow wingbeats of most satyrs create the impression these butterflies hop between strokes.

Little is known about the Guatemalan satyr, although DeVries reports they are widespread throughout virtually all Costa Rican forest habitats and are commonly sighted on the periphery of wooded areas. The adult butterfly's forewing length is approximately ¾ to 8/10 inch (18 to 21 mm).

Females lay black eggs singly on grasses such as *Eleusine* at the foot of a tree. Mature caterpillars are bright green and sport two tails at the rear and a pair of red horns on the head; the chrysalis is pale green and smooth. Adult Guatemalan satyrs seem to prefer sap, rotting fruit, and fungi; one individual kept in an insectary lived more than four months, surprising scientists who estimated the average lifespan of this small butterfly would be, at best, a few weeks.

Sweet oil butterfly

Mechanitis polymnia

The sweet oil butterfly is known by another name—the disturbed tigerwing—in some parts of its range from Mexico to the Amazon Basin. "The disturbed tigerwing is not upset by nature," Cassie explains. "It derives its common name from the fact that it frequents many more disturbed habitats than most ithomiine butterflies." Since these habitats (clear-cut forests and scorched pasture-land) are invariably disturbed by humans, *Mechanitis* species are usually found near civilization, even in the streets of some cities. This species flies in direct sunshine as well as shade, and its preferred sanctuaries are "dank, gloomy gullies" with high humidity, Ken Preston-Mafham reports.

Tigerwings belong to a notorious Neotropical mimicry ring that both fascinates and frustrates researchers. In the tiger-stripe complex—one of five mimicry rings originally recognized by the English naturalist Henry Bates—a broad assortment of long-winged butterflies (and a few daytime moths) mimic one another. Their forewings sport bold orange-and-yellow stripes, some straight, others wavy, alongside brown or black; their hindwings are mostly orange, punctuated with a dark bar or spots and dark wing margins.

From cocoon forth a butterfly
As lady from her door
Emerged—a summer afternoon—
Repairing everywhere.

Without design, that I could trace,
Except to stray abroad
On miscellaneous enterprise
The clovers understood....

—Emily Dickinson, "From Cocoon Forth a Butterfly," *Complete Poems* (1924)

Sweet oil butterfly
The sweet oil butterfly is a member of the Neotropical tiger-stripe mimicry complex, a ring of unrelated butterflies and moths that bear an extraordinary resemblance to one another. Caterpillars of this species feed on deadly nightshade, which confers protection to the model as well as its mimics.

All five mimicry rings are composed of Müllerian mimics, defined as unrelated unpalatable butterflies that benefit from their close resemblance to one another. These rings are found in the same habitat, although each complex may fly at a different level above ground, "thereby minimizing contact with the others in the fellowship of the ring but benefiting from predators' unwillingness to re-encounter distasteful prey," says Preston-Mafham. *Mechanitis polymnia*, he suspects, is likely one of the central models in its complex.

The sweet oil butterfly has a wingspan of 2½ to 3¼ inches (6 to 8 cm). Adults are attracted to mistflowers, among others, and females lay eggs in clusters chiefly on solanum hostplants—herbs, vines, and woody shrubs in the nightshade family. *Mechanitis* caterpillars are pale green and have a skirt of prominent protuberances on their sides. When feeding on leaves of nightshade-family tomato plants, the gregarious caterpillars are able to thwart the tomato's minute hooked spines by spinning fine webs to cover them. Chrysalides are shiny gold or silver and reflect the colors of their immediate surroundings.

Long-tailed skipper

Urbanus proteus

The long-tailed skipper has the requisite thick, hairy body of a skipper, but it also sports a prominent pair of hindwing tails not unlike those of a luna moth. There are several genera of long-tailed skippers, but in North America *Urbanus proteus* is the most common longtail and the only one with iridescent blue-green on its wings and body.

This skipper's wings are a dark chocolate, with silvery-white or glassy spots on the forewings and metallic blue-green hairs at the base. The underside of the wings is a complex pale-brown pattern with dark outer bands. The long-tailed skipper has a large, stout body, and its antennae have a skipper's characteristically curved or boomerang-shaped tips.

Ranging from the lower southeastern United States and southern Texas through the tropical Americas to Argentina, the long-tailed skipper regularly migrates northward in spring up the Atlantic seacoast, into the Mississippi Valley (sometimes to Illinois and Michigan), and westward to southern Arizona and California. According to Holland, it was once seen as far north as New York City and was even collected in Central Park. This longtail has a wingspan of 1½ to 2 inches (3.8 to 5.2 cm) and is a fast and erratic flyer.

Favored habitats include open fields, woodland margins, thorn forests, roadsides, fencerows, and along paths, clearings, and riverbanks. Adults are avid nectar seekers and show a preference for lantana and flowers of Spanish needle. But the most popular attraction for longtails is a cultivated bean patch, where viny legumes such as garden snap beans and butterfly peas serve as larval host-plants. The caterpillars are agricultural pests, and large infestations can seriously damage farmers' bean crops.

Males perch in sunlit areas, where they wait for prospective mates; females lay clusters of up to about ten pale-yellow eggs on the underside of leaves. Southern farmers call the caterpillars "bean leaf rollers" and "roller worms" in reference to their distinctive nests, which are constructed by tying leaves or pieces of leaves together with strands of silk. The yellow- or olive-green caterpillars have black heads with orange eyespots and lateral stripes of yellow, red, black, and green. The chrysalis is brown and covered with white wax.

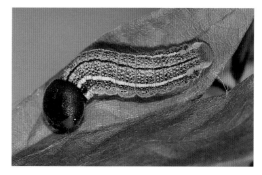

Long-tailed skipper caterpillar
The larvae of long-tailed skippers can be serious pests. Nicknamed the bean leaf roller or roller worm, the yellow-green caterpillar creates a refuge by drawing together the edges of a bean or pea leaf or by stitching together overlapping leaves.

The skipper is like a terrifically powered, supersonic fighter plane with its wings cut down to a minimum.

—Alexander B. and Elsie B. Klots, *Living Insects of the World* (1975)

Long-tailed skipper
The long-tailed skipper is a robust, dark-bodied butterfly whose long hindwing tails offer conveniently expendable targets as a defense against predators.

Chapter 4

Butterfly Conservation

Butterflies, says biologist Michael Samways, act as the "flamboyant flagships" of insect conservation. While insects and other invertebrates rarely share the spotlight with their more "charismatic" vertebrate brethren (whales, pandas, and tigers, for example), butterflies offer star quality and glamour that moths, beetles, and gnats cannot bring to the table. Their higher profile is a good thing, because the insect world needs an icon. Many habitats populated by butterflies and other insects are currently being degraded, fragmented, or destroyed—but the public has yet to take notice.

Like frogs, whose populations in the United States and abroad went into abrupt decline in the 1990s, butterflies are highly vulnerable to environmental change. And, like frogs, butterflies today are being touted as "canaries in the coal mine"—early-warning bioindicators that are sensitive to disruption by human activity and that may portend a dire outcome for other insects, wild creatures, and humans.

In 2002, English entomologist David Carter declared that butterfly populations had "decreased alarmingly" in many parts of the world. Two years later, ecologists reported in the journal *Science* that butterfly extinction rates in Great Britain and elsewhere were similar to those of larger, better-studied animals, and they warned that butterfly species were "crashing world-wide." The sheer numbers of these insects, experts had always presumed, would protect them from extinction. But the "gloomy result" of their research was that butterflies had "declined massively." A large die-off, lead author Jeremy Thomas told *Nature*, would be "bad news for global diversity."

Dwindling butterfly populations—once discounted because of expected seasonal fluctuations—now alarm scientists around the world. Just because butterflies can take wing and deposit eggs in more than one location doesn't mean they're safe from environmental threats: their fragility and susceptibility to habitat deterioration, not to mention natural catastrophes and climate change, account for an undeniable crisis.

Atala
Florida's once-abundant atala, or coontie hairstreak (*Eumaeus atala*), was decimated by commercial harvesting of coontie plants for starch and encroachment by developers into coastal habitats. Conservationists rallied support to save the butterfly by providing potted plants for egg-laying females in the last-known atala colony, then dispersing the hostplants across its former range.

It's hard to learn about animals if you only see them dead on dissecting trays.

—Diane Ackerman, "The Winter Palace of Monarchs," *Rarest of the Rare* (1995)

Currently, forty-five species are listed under the U.S. Endangered Species Act as endangered or threatened; internationally, the World Conservation Union's IUCN Red Data Book cites more than twenty. Already declared extinct in England are the large copper (*Lycaena dispar dispar*) and large blue (*Maculinea arion*); in California, a subspecies of the American apollo (*Parnassius clodius strohbeeni*); and, in San Francisco, the Xerces blue (*Glaucopsyche xerces*) and Boisduval's satyr (*Cercyonis sthenele*).

Among those near extinction or extirpated in certain Florida localities are the Miami blue (*Hemiargus thomasi*), atala (*Eumaeus atala*), and Schaus' swallowtail (*Papilio aristodemus*); in Colorado, Minor's swallowtail (*P. indra minori*); in the eastern United States, Mitchell's satyr (*Neonympha mitchellii*); in California, the San Francisco bay checkerspot (*Euphydryas editha bayensis*), El Segundo blue (*Euphilotes bernardino allyni*), and Palos Verdes blue (*Glaucopsyche lygdamus palosverdesensis*); in Ontario and the northeastern United States, the Karner blue (*Lycaeides melissa samuelis*); in Jamaica, the Homerus swallowtail (*P. homerus*); and in Papua New Guinea, Queen Alexandra's birdwing (*Ornithoptera alexandrae*), Cairn's birdwing (*O. priamus*), and other birdwings.

Although many conservation-minded citizens presume that collectors pose the greatest threat to butterflies (and some rare birdwings do command $7,500 a pair on the black market), scientists agree that habitat damage poses a far more critical danger. Because many species lay their eggs on a single variety of hostplant, environmental encroachment by humans can have horrendous consequences. Many factors contribute to the degradation, fragmentation, and destruction of local habitats, effectively altering the balance of nature. These include industrial, residential, and agricultural development; road construction; logging; mining; water diversion and dams; wetlands drainage; prairie burning; overgrazing; and the introduction of intrusive plants and predatory or competitive animal species. Next come the deadly chemicals: pesticides to control mosquitoes and agricultural pests but fatal to butterflies as well; herbicides to kill weeds along roadsides and in gardens but which also decimate hostplants and nectar sources; and genetically engineered crops such as corn that kill monarch caterpillars when the toxins intended for corn borers are spread by airborne pollen to nearby milkweeds. In addition, all manner of contaminants and chemical pollutants now turn up in the water and air.

Natural calamities also aggravate biodegradation. Forest fires, earthquakes, and pestilence take their toll, but particularly destructive are weather-related disasters such as hurricanes, tornadoes, flooding, drought, freezing temperatures, and ice storms, some of which are exacerbated by climate change and global warming. Population biologist Camille Parmesan, who has studied the impact of climate change on North American and European butterflies with particular emphasis on Edith's checkerspot (*Euphydryas editha*), contends that "these trends bear a human fingerprint." Now nearly extinct in Mexico, Edith's checkerspot has been shifting its range northward to Canada due to increasing weather extremes on the hot and dry end of the spectrum.

"Climate change is fundamentally different from other causes of extinction, because it is the only one you cannot locally do anything about," Parmesan told environmental writer Alex Shoumatoff. On the other hand, global warming—caused by carbon dioxide in the atmosphere—is "the thing that the individual can do the most about...like trading in their SUV for a Honda Civic that gets 40 miles per gallon," she continued. "If everyone just did that, it would make a huge dent."

Like checkerspots, monarchs are affected by climate. Every fall, they migrate by the millions to Mexico or the Pacific coast to escape subfreezing temperatures farther north. Roosting on oyamel firs in Mexico or non-native eucalyptus in California, monarchs are sheltered by trees with big trunks, which retain more warmth. Illegal logging in the Mexican sanctuaries by bands of armed mafia, which chop down as many as seventy mature trees per day, threatens overwintering monarchs by exposing them to extreme cold. In 1981, a freeze killed some 2.5 million adults; in 1995, a snowstorm wiped out 30 million adults; and in 2002, a rainstorm followed by a sudden freeze soaked and froze more than a quarter of a billion adult monarchs. Severe storms in early 2004 reduced the overwintering population to the lowest recorded numbers in recent years, according to Monarch Watch.

Biologists Lincoln Brower and Robert Pyle proposed an innovative category of international protection for migrating monarchs—not in and of themselves an endangered species—which they dubbed "threatened phenomena"; in 1983, the IUCN formally accepted their designation. Yet pressures on

migratory monarchs remain enormous. "Time is rapidly running out," Brower warns.

The extirpation of local and regional populations of butterflies is particularly serious, because some species have disappeared even while being protected. For example, Mitchell's satyrs seen annually in the fens of New Jersey were devastated not just by habitat change and encroaching development but also by brazen collectors who disregarded chain-link fences, guard dogs, and a security watchman. Urban development of coastal dune ecosystems in the San Francisco area eradicated at least three local species or subspecies and now threatens three others. The last-known Xerces blues were observed flying over wild lupine at the Presidio in 1943; shortly thereafter, their habitat was covered with gravel and built upon to accommodate military vehicles and weapons. (The Xerces Society, a nonprofit international invertebrate conservation organization, was named for this species.) The saga of the Palos

Atala caterpillars
Once nearly extinct, the atala butterfly has made a dramatic comeback in Florida. Sustained by the newly established patches of coontie, these bright red-and-yellow atala caterpillars—sporting vivid warning colors—eagerly devour the young leaves of their favored hostplant.

Verdes blue ends more encouragingly: although declared officially extinct in 1983, this subspecies was rediscovered in 1994 by workers clearing brush alongside Navy fuel-storage tanks near Los Angeles International Airport. The Navy built a small on-site lab where environmentalists could breed the blues, and scientists and a former gang member who volunteered to work with the L.A. Conservation Corps were later recognized for their contributions to preserving the butterfly.

Another environmental-rescue story involves the Miami blue, a species once abundant in South Florida. It was so decimated by coastal development, habitat loss, and mosquito spraying that the final remaining colonies retreated to the Florida Keys. In 1992, according to Glassberg, Hurricane Andrew obliterated the last known colony (on Key Biscayne), and no Miami blues were seen for years. Then, in 1999, a sharp-eyed observer sent images that she had photographed on Bahia Honda Key to Glassberg, and after confirming they were Miami blues, he successfully petitioned the state to declare the butterfly an endangered species—with a $5,000 fine and jail time for anyone who harmed the insect.

Nonetheless, most threatened butterflies fare far less well—and no one knows for sure just how many species, especially in tropical zones, have vanished over the last century or so. "The notion that collecting and killing animals, for whatever reason, could be in any way morally wrong was not an issue until quite recent times," authority Michael Salmon argues in his book about British butterfly collectors. "The real threat to rare or local species was excessive trading that lacked all purpose other than monetary gain....Such excesses are largely a thing of the past." To be sure, butterfly farms and ranches in Central America, Madagascar, and China, modeled after successful ventures in Papua New Guinea, can discourage trade in unlawfully obtained specimens—especially among the more reckless dealers and customers in the United States, Germany, and Japan—while at the same time providing natives with an incentive to preserve their tropical habitats.

But effective butterfly conservation requires many things, including more purposeful efforts by educators and the media to inform the public and their elected officials; tougher environmental laws and stiffer enforcement and sanctions; greater trust and teamwork between bureaucracies (federal, state, and local) and scientists; and a change in attitudes and behavior.

Citizens who value butterflies—and who recognize the urgency to protect them and their habitats *now* rather than after it's too late—can do something. They can join or donate money to environmental, scientific, and educational organizations; plant butterfly gardens with hostplants preferred by caterpillars and nectar sources sought by adults; participate in seasonal tagging projects and local census counts; challenge the planting of genetically modified corn and other crops; reduce or halt the use of pesticides in their yards and community; elect lawmakers who publicly support the Endangered Species Act and who vote to fund measures promoting habitat preservation and a healthier environment; keep an eye on federal and

state agencies charged with safeguarding the nation's natural resources; encourage educators to include natural history, biology, and ecology in school curricula and on field trips; read and share pertinent information; and resist the impulse to overcollect butterflies when shooting photographs and studying museum-mounted specimens should satisfy the same urge to appreciate butterflies up close.

"Nature is part of us, as we are part of nature," the eminent entomologist E. O. Wilson has written. Conservation should be part of us, too—especially if we wish future generations to enjoy butterflies just as we do today.

Monarchs

Seasonal migrations of monarchs are monitored by environmental organizations such as Monarch Watch, as well as by scientists, students, and ordinary citizens. Every fall, thousands of monarchs migrate to this protected grove in Pismo Beach, California, and overwinter from October to February.

Chapter 5

Butterfly Photography

"This is a great time to photograph butterflies," declares Brian Kenney, who shot every picture in this book. The reason? New digital cameras provide instant feedback, permitting photographers to adjust exposures on the spot if a picture doesn't work and to shoot virtually unlimited photos at no additional cost once the camera itself is paid for. "For dinosaurs like me who are still shooting film," he adds, "the sharpness, speed, and saturation of today's films put those of a few years back to shame." Modern flashes feature more power and greater control, he points out, "and autofocus, image stabilization, and macro lenses have revolutionized butterfly photography."

But is it necessary to acquire newer, more expensive equipment to take great pictures? "Actually, the cameras and flashes I normally use for macrophotography haven't been made for years," Kenney admits, "and I would challenge anyone to tell which pictures were taken with the older equipment and which were taken with the newest. There is absolutely no difference in the quality of the images."

Most of the photos in this book—shot over a period of roughly twenty years—were taken with an "ancient" Nikon N8008s camera body and either a 105mm f2.8 or a 200mm f4 macro lens. Kenney prefers Fuji Sensia and Provia 100ASA 35mm slide film "because the color balance of the pictures seems to match what my eye sees more closely." He uses Fuji Velvia and Kodak E100VS slide film for some subjects and longer telephoto lenses "when I need greater working distance to approach a wary subject." Also helpful for getting the magnification and quality of lighting that he wants are multipliers, close-up diopters (supplementary lenses), polarizers, extension tubes, tripods, macro sliders, clamps, handmade flash brackets, flash cords, slaves, and up to three flashes.

"But, in the end," Kenney insists, "a camera is just a box to hold film—or equivalent digital media. Butterfly photography isn't about the equipment; the whole point is your personal connection to these incredible winged wonders."

Zebra longwings
A male zebra longwing (*Heliconius charitonius*) engages in a behavior known as "mate guarding." The male beats his wings over a rival's head and body, hoping to drive his competitor away from a virgin female soon to emerge from her chrysalis. Shot with natural light augmented by fill flash, using a 200mm f4 macro lens (1/30 second @ f4).

Float like a butterfly, sting like a bee.

—Muhammad Ali, boxing credo devised by aide Drew "Bundini" Brown

Photographing butterflies

The photographer takes pictures of zebra longwings mate-guarding a chrysalis. Stretched out at eye level with his subjects, a photographer can achieve dramatically different effects by selecting different combinations of depth of field, shutter speed, focal length, and full flash versus fill flash and/or natural light. The two other pictures in this chapter were both taken from this position. If you look closely, you can see the butterflies just to the right of the photographer. (*Photograph by Joyce Sprenger*)

Kenney's advice for finding subjects to shoot is to plant a backyard butterfly garden. "When the mood strikes you," he suggests, "wander outside with camera in hand and try your luck at capturing the action. Experience is the best teacher." Once you've mastered the basics, he urges, visit a butterfly conservatory and "go wild." And then consider going farther afield—"if you dare."

"There is nothing like the sight of morpho butterflies flying low over a babbling brook in the montane rainforests of Costa Rica," he rhapsodizes, "their brilliant blue wings flashing in the sunlight, winking on and off as the wings open and close." Kenney has also photographed at the butterfly reserve in Michoacán, Mexico, where monarchs overwinter. "From a distance, the mountainside seems ablaze with a strange, cold fire, but, as you approach, the mass of orange resolves into millions of individual butterflies clinging to the trees and completely overwhelming the colors of the natural foliage." Although short of breath from climbing the steep trail at a very high altitude, Kenney recalls he could hear "the soft rhythmic sound" of their wings as the butterflies took flight.

Specialty lenses, such as Canon's 1x-5x 60mm macro lens, allow photographers to easily shoot caterpillars and eggs at extreme magnifications. And flash can be absolutely critical. Butterflies are diurnal, so pictures "should look like they were taken in natural daylight," he says. That usually involves fill flash, to avoid potentially distracting shadows and bring out the iridescent colors on a butterfly's wings.

Kenney shot many of his subjects with a hand-held camera, but if they remained in one place long enough, he used a tripod. "I don't personally use autofocus for macrophotography," he comments. "I find it easier to prefocus the lens and lean in and out until the subject is in sharp focus. Even the most modern cameras tend to lose autofocus lock or focus on the wrong point when confronted with the narrow depths of field encountered in macrophotography."

Despite suffering from altitude sickness, parasites, brutal heat, and "camera-destroying humidity" while pursuing butterflies, Kenney has few regrets. "A hundred years ago, I might have gone afield with net in hand and baggage filled with killing jars. Today, the trophies are pictures, and the subjects fly free. The challenge is in the chase, and the reward is seeing a side of the natural world that few experience in their lifetimes."

Zebra longwings

In this photograph, the male zebra longwing guarding a prospective mate folds his wings around the female's chrysalis to prevent his rival from landing. Shot with full TTL flash using a 105mm f2.8 macro lens and two flashes (1/250 second @ f16). Full flash was necessary here to stop the action and ensure sufficient depth of field for both butterflies to be in focus.

Butterfly Organizations and Exhibits

Butterfly Organizations

Association of Tropical Lepidoptera
Gainesville, Florida
www.troplep.org

The Australian Entomological Society
Orange, Australia
www.agric.nsw.gov.au/Hort/ascu/myrmecia/society.htm

Butterfly Conservation Society
Wareham, Dorset, United Kingdom
www.butterfly-conservation.org

Butterfly Lovers International
San Francisco, California

Entomological Society of Canada
Ottawa, Canada
www.esc-sec.org

The Lepidopterists' Society
Los Angeles, California
www.lepsoc.org

North American Butterfly Association
Morristown, New Jersey
www.naba.org

Southern Lepidopterists' Society
Pisgah Forest, North Carolina
www.southernlepsoc.org

Xerces Society
Portland, Oregon
www.xerces.org

National Butterfly Exhibits

Please contact the exhibit before planning a visit. Many butterfly exhibits are seasonal and may not be open year-round. Contact information was accurate at the time of the book's publication, but the publisher cannot assume responsibility for changes.

Alabama

Biophilia Nature Center
Elberta, Alabama
334-987-1200
www.biophilia.net

Tessman Butterfly House
Huntsville, Alabama
256-830-4447
www.hsvbg.org/bflies.htm

California

Butterfly Exhibit at Turtle Bay Museum and
    Arboretum
Redding, California
530-243-8850
www.turtlebay.org

Butterfly Habitat at Six Flags Marine World
Vallejo, California
707-644-4000
www.sixflags.com/marineworld

Robinsons-May Pavilion of Wings Butterfly
    House
Los Angeles, California
213-763-3558
www.nhm.org

San Diego Wild Animal Park
Escondido, California
760-738-5077
www.sandiegozoo.org

Colorado

Butterfly Pavilion and Insect Center
Westminster, Colorado
303-469-5441
www.butterflies.org

Western Colorado Botanical Gardens and
    Butterfly House
Grand Junction, Colorado
970-245-3288
www.wcbotanic.org

Delaware

Butterfly House at the Ashland Nature Center
Hockessin, Delaware
302-239-2334
www.delawarenaturesociety.org

District of Columbia

Pollinarium at the National Zoological Park
Washington, D.C.
202-673-4789
http://natzoo.si.edu

Florida

Butterfly Exhibit at the Brevard Zoo
Melbourne, Florida
321-254-9453
www.brevardzoo.org

Butterfly Rainforest at the Florida Museum
    of Natural History
Gainesville, Florida
353-846-2000
www.flmnh.ufl.edu

Butterfly World
Coconut Creek, Florida
305-977-4434
www.butterflyworld.com

Cypress Gardens Wings of Wonder
Winter Haven, Florida
941-324-2111
www.cypressgardens.com

Key West Butterfly and Nature Conservatory
Key West, Florida
800-839-4647
www.keywestbutterfly.com

Lukas Butterfly Encounter
Oviedo, Florida
407-365-6163
www.lukasnursery.com

Georgia

Cecil B. Day Butterfly Center at Callaway
    Gardens
Pine Mountain, Georgia
706-663-5102
www.callawaygardens.com

Illinois

"Butterflies!" at the Brookfield Zoo
Brookfield, Illinois
708-485-0263
www.brookfieldzoo.org

Judy Istock Butterfly Haven
Chicago, Illinois
773-755-5100
www.chias.org

Indiana

Indianapolis Zoo
Indianapolis, Indiana
317-630-2034
www.indyzoo.com

Iowa

Christina Reiman Butterfly Wing at Iowa
    State University
Ames, Iowa
515-294-2567
www.reimangardens.iastate.edu

Kansas

Botanica's Butterfly House
Wichita, Kansas
316-264-0448
www.botanica.org

Kentucky

Butterfly Exhibit at the Louisville Zoo
Louisville, Kentucky
502-238-5614
www.louisvillezoo.org

Louisiana

Butterflies in Flight at the Audubon Insectarium
New Orleans, Louisiana
504-861-6170
www.auduboninstitute.org

Maryland

Brookside Gardens
Wheaton, Maryland
301-929-6506
www.brooksidegardens.org

Massachusetts

Butterfly Landing at Zoo New England
Boston, Massachusetts
617-989-2064
www.zoonewengland.com

The Butterfly Place
Westford, Massachusetts
508-392-0955
www.butterflyplace-ma.com

Magic Wings
South Deerfield, Massachusetts
413-665-2805
www.magicwings.com

Michigan

Detroit Zoological Institute Butterfly Exhibit
Royal Oak, Michigan
248-398-0903
www.detroitzoo.org

Dow Gardens
Midland, Michigan
517-631-2677
www.dowgardens.org

Lena Meijer Conservatory at the Frederik
    Meijer Gardens
Grand Rapids, Michigan
616-977-7680
www.meijergardens.org

Wings of Mackinac
Mackinac Island, Michigan
906-847-9464
www.wingsofmackinac.com

Minnesota

Butterfly Garden at the Minnesota Zoo
Apple Valley, Minnesota
952-431-9500
www.mnzoo.com

Missouri

The Butterfly Place
Branson, Missouri
417-332-2231
www.butterflyplace.com

Mary Ann Lee Butterfly Wing at the Saint Louis Zoo
Saint Louisv, Missouri
314-781-0900
www.stlzoo.org

Sophia M. Sachs Butterfly House
Chesterfield, Missouri
636-530-0076
www.butterflyhouse.org

Nebraska

The Butterfly Pavilion at the Lincoln Children's
    Zoo and Botanical Gardens
Lincoln, Nebraska
402-475-6741
www.lincolnzoo.org

New York

The Butterfly Conservatory at the American
  Museum of Natural History
New York, New York
212-496-3583
www.amnh.org

Butterfly Vivarium at the Sweetbriar Nature
  Center
Smithtown, New York
516-265-2100
www.sweetbriarnc.org

Butterfly Zone at the Bronx Zoo
Bronx, New York
718-220-5098
www.bronxzoo.com

Up Yonda Farm Environmental Education
  Center
Bolton Landing, New York
518-644-9767
www.upyondafarm.com

North Carolina

The Living Conservatory and Arthropod Zoo
  at the North Carolina Museum of Natural
  Sciences
Raleigh, North Carolina
919-733-7450
www.naturalsciences.org

Magic Wings Butterfly House at the North
  Carolina Museum of Life & Science
Durham, North Carolina
919-220-5429
www.ncmls.org

Ohio

Butterfly House
Whitehouse, Ohio
419-877-2733
www.butterfly-house.com

Cleveland Metroparks Zoo
Cleveland, Ohio
216-635-3335
www.clemetzoo.com

Insect World's Aviary at the Cincinnati Zoo
  Insectarium
Cincinnati, Ohio
513-281-4701
www.cincyzoo.org

Krohn Conservatory
Cincinnati, Ohio
513-421-5707
www.cinci-parks.org

Oklahoma

Wings of Wonder at the Tulsa Zoo and
  Living Museum
Tulsa, Oklahoma
918-669-6600
www.tulsazoo.org

Oregon

Butterflies Forever
Astoria, Oregon
503-738-3180
www.oregonbutterflies.org

Winged Wonders Butterfly Exhibit at
  the Oregon Zoo
Portland, Oregon
www.oregonzoo.org

Pennsylvania

Academy of Natural Sciences
Philadelphia, Pennsylvania
215-299-1034
www.acnatsci.org

Butterfly Forest at the Phipps Conservatory
  and Botanical Gardens
Pittsburgh, Pennsylvania
412-622-6914
www.conservatory.org

Hershey Gardens Butterfly House
Hershey, Pennsylvania
717-534-3493
www.hersheygardens.org

South Carolina

The Butterfly House at Cypress Gardens
Moncks Corner, South Carolina
843-553-0515
www.cypressgardens.org

South Dakota

Sertoma Butterfly House
Sioux Falls, South Dakota
605-334-9466
www.sertomabutterflyhouse.org

Texas

The Butterfly Haus at Wildseed Farm
Fredericksburg, Texas
800-848-0078
www.wildseedfarms.com

Cockrell Butterfly Center at the Houston
  Museum of Natural History
Houston, Texas
713-639-4678
www.hmns.org

House of Butterflies
Waxahachie, Texas
972-333-1653
www.houseofbutterflies.org

NABA International Butterfly Park
Mission, Texas
www.naba.org/nababp

Rosine Smith Sammons Butterfly House
  at Texas Discovery Gardens
Dallas, Texas
214-428-7476
www.texasdiscoverygardens.org

Washington

Butterflies and Blooms at the Woodland
  Park Zoo
Seattle, Washington
206-684-4836
www.zoo.org

Tropical Butterfly House and Insect Village
  at the Pacific Science Center
Seattle, Washington
206-443-2905
www.pacsci.org

Wisconsin

Puelicher Butterfly Wing at the Milwaukee
  Public Museum
Milwaukee, Wisconsin
414-278-6936
www.mpm.edu

International Butterfly Exhibits

Australia

Australia Butterfly Sanctuary
Kuranda, Queensland, Australia
61-7-4093-7575
www.australianbutterflies.com

Coffs Harbour Butterfly House
Bonville, New South Wales, Australia
61-2-6653-4766
www.butterflyhouse.com.au

The Butterfly House at the Royal Melbourne
   Zoological Gardens
Parkville, Victoria, Australia
61-3-9285-9300
www.zoo.org.au

Canada

Butterfly World and Gardens Coombs
Coombs, British Columbia, Canada
250-248-7026
www.nature-world.com

Butterfly Exhibit at the Calgary Zoo
Calgary, Alberta, Canada
403-294-7661
www.calgaryzoo.org

Niagara Parks Butterfly Conservatory
Niagara Falls, Ontario, Canada
905-356-8554
www.niagaraparks.com

Victoria Butterfly Garden
Brentwood Bay, British Columbia, Canada
250-652-3822
www.butterflygardens.com

Costa Rica

The Butterfly Farm
La Guacima, Alajuela, Costa Rica
506-438-0400
www.butterflyfarm.co.cr

Italy

Butterfly Arc
Montegrotto Terme, Padova, Italy
39-0498910189
www.butterflyarc.it

Malaysia

Penang Butterfly Farm
Penang, Malaysia
60-4-4-8851253
www.butterfly-insect.com

Spain

Butterfly Park Empuriabrava
Castello d'empuries, Spain
34-972450761
www.butterflyparkinfo.com

United Kingdom

Edinburgh Butterfly & Insect World
Midlothian, Scotland, United Kingdom
44-0131-663-4932
www.edinburgh-butterfly-world.co.uk

Stratford-upon-Avon Butterfly Farm and Jungle Safari
Warwickshire, England, United Kingdom
44-1789-299288
www.butterflyfarm.co.uk

Common buckeye
The common buckeye (*Junonia coenia*) is a familiar summer visitor to most of the continental United States.

Bibliography

Ackery, P. R., R. de Jong, and R. I. Vane-Wright. "Taxonomy of Butterflies: The Scale of the Problem—Numbers of species by family and subfamily." Butterfly Taxome Project: Butterfly Families, www.ucl.ac.uk/taxome/rhopnos.html. From "The Butterflies." In *Handbuch der Zoologie*, edited by N. P. Kristensen, 263–300. Part 35. Berlin: W. de Gruyter, 1999.

Ackery, P. R., and R. I. Vane-Wright. *Milkweed Butterflies: Their Cladistics and Biology*. London: British Museum of Natural History; Ithaca, NY: Cornell University Press, 1984.

Ajilvsgi, Geyata. *Butterfly Gardening for the South*. Dallas: Taylor Publishing, 1990.

Allen, Thomas J., Jim P. Brock, and Jeffrey Glassberg. *Caterpillars in the Field and Garden*. New York: Oxford University Press, 2005.

Arnett, Ross H., Jr. *American Insects: A Handbook of the Insects of America North of Mexico*. 2nd ed. Boca Raton, FL: CRC Press, 2000.

Baker, Christopher P. *Costa Rica Handbook*. Chico, CA: Moon Publications, 1994.

Barker, Will. *Familiar Insects of America*. New York: Harper & Brothers, 1960.

Boggs, Carol L., Ward B. Watt, and Paul R. Ehrlich, eds. *Butterflies: Ecology and Evolution Taking Flight*. Chicago: University of Chicago Press, 2003.

Braby, Michael F. *Butterflies of Australia: Their Identification, Biology and Distribution*. Two vols. Collingwood, Australia: CSIRO Publishing, 2000.

Brewer, Jo. *Butterflies*. Photographs by Kjell B. Sandved. New York: Abrams, 1978.

Brock, Jim P., and Kenn Kaufman. *Butterflies of North America*. Boston: Houghton Mifflin, 2003.

Brower, Lincoln P. "Monarchs." In *Encyclopedia of Insects*, edited by Vincent H. Resh and Ring T. Cardé, 739–743. Burlington, MA: Academic Press, 2003.

Buchmann, Stephen L., and Gary Paul Nabhan. "Need Nectar, Will Travel." In *Insect Lives: Stories of Mystery and Romance From a Hidden World*, edited by Erich Hoyt and Ted Schultz, 127–130. New York: John Wiley & Sons, 1999.

Butterflies: Pocket Guide. London: Quantum Publishing, 2004.

Carter, David. *Smithsonian Handbook of Butterflies and Moths*. Photography by Frank Greenaway. New York: Dorling Kindersley, 2002.

Cassie, Brian. *A World of Butterflies*. Photographs by Kjell Sandved. New York: Bullfinch Press, 2004.

Common, I. F. B., and D. F. Waterhouse. *Butterflies of Australia*. Sydney, Australia: Angus & Robertson, 1972.

Comstock, John H., and Anna B. Comstock. *How to Know the Butterflies: A Manual of Those Which Occur in the Eastern United States*. Ithaca, NY: Comstock Publishing, 1943.

D'Abrera, Bernard. *Butterflies of the Australian Region*. Melbourne, Australia: Lansdowne, 1971.

———. *Butterflies of the Afrotropical Region*. Melbourne, Australia: Lansdowne, 1980.

———. *Butterflies of the Oriental Region*. Part 1, *Papilionidae, Pierida, & Danaidae*. Victoria, Australia: Hill House, 1982.

———. *Butterflies of the Oriental Region*. Part 2, *Nymphalidae, Satyridae & Amathusidae*. Victoria, Australia: Hill House, 1985.

———. *Butterflies of the Oriental Region*. Part 3, *Lycaenidae & Riodinidae*. Victoria, Australia: Hill House, 1986.

Daccordi, Mauro, Paolo Triberti, and Adriano Zanetti. *Simon & Schuster's Guide to Butterflies & Moths*. New York: Simon & Schuster/Fireside, 1987.

Daniels, Jaret C. *Butterflies of Florida Field Guide*. Cambridge, MN: Adventure Publications, 2003.

Dempster, Jack P. "The Natural Enemies of Butterflies." In *The Biology of Butterflies*, edited by R. I. Vane-Wright and P. R. Ackery, 97–104. London: Academic Press, 1984.

DeVries, Philip J. *The Butterflies of Costa Rica and Their Natural History*. Vol. 1, *Papilionidae, Pieridae, Nymphalidae*. Princeton, NJ: Princeton University Press, 1987.

———. *The Butterflies of Costa Rica and Their Natural History*. Vol. 2, *Riodinidae*. Princeton, NJ: Princeton University Press, 1997.

Dickens, Michael. *The World of Butterflies*. New York: Macmillan, 1971.

Dickerson, Mary C. *Moths and Butterflies*. Boston: Ginn & Company, 1901.

Dillard, Annie. *Pilgrim at Tinker Creek*. New York: Bantam, 1975.

Dingle, Hugh. "Migration." In *Encyclopedia of Insects*, edited by Vincent H. Resh and Ring T. Cardé, 708–714. San Diego, CA: Academic Press, 2003.

Douglas, Matthew M. *The Lives of Butterflies*. Ann Arbor: University of Michigan Press, 1986.

Eisner, Thomas. *For Love of Insects*. Cambridge, MA: Belknap Press of Harvard University Press, 2003.

Emmel, Thomas C. *Butterflies: Their World, Their Life Cycle, Their Behavior*. New York: Alfred A. Knopf, 1975.

———. *Florida's Fabulous Butterflies*. Photographs by Brian Kenney. Tampa, FL: World Publications, 1997.

Evans, Howard E. *The Pleasures of Entomology: Portraits of Insects and the People Who Study Them*. Washington, DC: Smithsonian Institution Press, 1985.

Fabre, J. Henri. *The Insect World of J. Henri Fabre*, edited by Edwin Way Teale. New York: Dodd, Mead, 1949.

Feltwell, John. *The Encyclopedia of Butterflies*. New York: Prentice Hall, 1993.

Ferris, Clifford D., and F. Martin Brown, eds. *Butterflies of the Rocky Mountain States*. Norman: University of Oklahoma Press, 1980.

Ford, E. B. *Butterflies*. London: Collins, 1957.

Fountaine, Margaret. *Love Among the Butterflies: The Travels and Adventures of a Victorian Lady*, edited by W. F. Cater. Boston: Little, Brown, 1980.

Glassberg, Jeffrey. *Butterflies Through Binoculars: The East*. New York: Oxford University Press, 1999.

———. "Saving South Florida's Butterflies: Miami Blue Fund." http://www.naba.org/miamiblue.html, December 5, 1999.

———. *Butterflies of North America*. New York: Barnes & Noble Books, 2004.

Goodden, Robert. *All Color Book of Butterflies*. London: Octopus Books, 1973.

Grimaldi, David, and Michael S. Engle. *Evolution of the Insects*. New York: Cambridge University Press, 2005.

Gwynne, Darryl. "Mating Behaviors." In *Encyclopedia of Insects*, edited by Vincent H. Resh and Ring T. Cardé, 682–688. San Diego, CA: Academic Press, 2003.

Halpern, Sue. *Four Wings and a Prayer*. New York: Vintage, 2002.

Hay-Roe, Mirian, and Richard Mankin. "Wing-Click Sounds of *Heliconius cydno alithea* (Nymphalidae: Heliconiinae) Butterflies." *Journal of Insect Behavior* 17, no. 3 (May 2004): 329–335.

Holland, W. J. *The Butterfly Book*. Revised edition. Garden, City, NY: Doubleday, 1949.

Hook, Patrick. *The World of Butterflies*. New York: Gramercy, 1999.

Horstman, Mark. "News in Science—Caterpillars fling faeces afar to fool foes." http://www.abc.net.au/science/news/stories/s822336.htm, February 4, 2003.

Hoyle, Martin, and Mike James. "Global Warming, Human Population, and Viability of the World's Smallest Butterfly." *Conservation Biology* 19, no. 4 (August 2005): 1113–1124.

Howe, William H. *Our Butterflies and Moths*. North Kansas City, MO: True Color Publishing, 1963.

Imes, Rick. *The Practical Entomologist*. New York: Fireside Books, 1992.

Janzen, Daniel H., ed. *Costa Rican Natural History*. Chicago: University of Chicago Press, 1983.

Johnson, Kurt, and Steve Coates. *Nabokov's Blues: The Scientific Odyssey of a Literary Genius*. Cambridge, MA: Zoland Books, 1999.

Joron, Mathieu. "Mimicry." In *Encyclopedia of Insects*, edited by Vincent H. Resh and Ring T. Cardé, 714–726. Burlington, MA: Academic Press, 2003.

Klots, Alexander B. *A Field Guide to the Butterflies of North America, East of the Great Plains*. Peterson Field Guide Series. Boston: Houghton Mifflin, 1951.

Klots, Alexander B., and Elsie B. Klots. *Living Insects of the World*. Garden City, NY: Doubleday, 1975.

Kricher, John. *A Neotropical Companion*. 2nd edition. Princeton, NJ: Princeton University Press, 1999.

Leach, Maria, ed. *Funk & Wagnalls Standard Dictionary of Folklore, Mythology, and Legend*. New York: Funk & Wagnalls, 1972. See esp. 176–177.

Lewis, H. L. *Butterflies of the World*. Chicago: Follett Publishing, 1973.

Linsenmaier, Walter. *Insects of the World*. Translated by Leigh E. Chadwick. New York: McGraw-Hill, 1972.

Manos-Jones, Maraleen. *The Spirit of Butterflies: Myth, Magic, and Art*. New York: Abrams, 2000.

Matthews, Patrick, ed. *The Pursuit of Moths and Butterflies: An Anthology*. London: Chatto & Windus, 1957.

Mikula, Rick. *Garden Butterflies of North America*. Minocqua, WI: Willow Creek Press, 1997.

Nabokov, Vladimir. "Nabokov's Butterflies." Edited by Brian Boyd. Translated by Dmitri Nabokov. *Atlantic Monthly*, April 2000, 51–75.

———. "Butterflies." In *Nature Writing: The Tradition in English*, edited by Robert Finch and John Elder, 423–432. New York: W. W. Norton, 2002.

Newman, L. Hugh. "Butterflies to Chartwell." In *Finest Hour*, 1989. The Churchill Centre Website, www.winstonchurchill.org/i4a/pages/index.cfm?pageid=413.

Nishida, Ritsuo. "Sequestration of Defensive Substances from Plants by Lepidoptera." *Annual Review of Entomology* 47 (2002): 57–92.

Oberhauser, Karen S., and Michelle J. Solensky, eds. *The Monarch Butterfly: Biology & Conservation*. Ithaca, NY: Cornell University Press, 2004.

Opler, Paul A. *Peterson Field Guide to Eastern Butterflies*. Boston: Houghton Mifflin, 1998.

Opler, Paul A., Harry Pavulaan, and Ray E. Stanford, coordinators. "Butterflies of North America." Northern Prairie Wildlife Research Center, www.npwrc.usgs.gov/resource.

Owen, D. F. *Tropical Butterflies: The Ecology and Behaviour of Butterflies in the Tropics with Special Reference to African Species*. Oxford: Clarendon Press, 1971.

Pain, Stephanie. "Sheer Brilliance." *New Scientist*, June 26, 1999, 3434.

Pence, J. Akers. "Longest Regularly Repeated Migration." Chap. 35 in *University of Florida Book of Insect Records*. http://ufbir.ifas.ufl.edu/chap35.htm, April 1998.

Porter, Keith. "A Kaleidoscope of Colors." In *Firefly Encyclopedia of Insects and Spiders*, edited by Christopher O'Toole, 170. Buffalo, NY: Firefly Books, 2002.

Powell, Jerry A. "Lepidoptera (Moths, Butterflies)." In *Encyclopedia of Insects*, Vincent H. Resh and Ring T. Cardé, 631–663. San Diego, CA: Academic Press, 2003.

Preston-Mafham, Ken. *Identifying Butterflies: The New Compact Study Guide and Identifier*. Edison, NJ: Chartwell Books, 1999.

Preston-Mafham, Rod, and Ken Preston-Mafham. *Butterflies of the World*. London: Blandford, 1999.

Pyle, Robert Michael. *Chasing Monarchs: Migrating with the Butterflies of Passage*. Boston: Mariner Books/Houghton Mifflin, 1999.

———. "Nabokov's Butterflies." *American Scholar* 69, no. 1 (Winter 2000): 95–110.

———. "Resurrection Ecology: Bring Back the Xerces Blue!" *Whole Earth*, Spring 2001, http://www.wholeearthmag.com/ArticleBin/421.html.

Resh, Vincent H., and Ring T. Cardé, eds. *Encyclopedia of Insects*. San Diego, CA: Academic Press, 2003.

Riley, Norman, ed. *Butterflies and Moths*. New York: Studio Books, 1965.

Russell, Sharman Apt. *An Obsession with Butterflies: Our Long Love Affair with a Singular Insect*. Cambridge, MA: Perseus Books, 2003.

Salmon, Michael A. *The Aurealian Legacy: British Butterflies and Their Collectors*. Berkeley: University of California Press, 2000.

Sbordoni, Valerio, and Saverio Forestiero. *Butterflies of the World*. Buffalo, NY: Firefly Books, 1998.

Schappert, Phil. *A World for Butterflies: Their Lives, Behavior and Future*. Buffalo, NY: Firefly Books, 2000.

Schwartz, Albert. *The Butterflies of Hispaniola*. Gainesville: University of Florida Press, 1989.

Scott, James A. *The Butterflies of North America: A Natural History and Field Guide*. Stanford, CA: Stanford University Press, 1986.

Sharp, David. *The Cambridge Natural History: Insects*. Vol. 2. 1911. Reprint, New York: Dover, 1970.

Shoumatoff, Alex. "Madame Butterfly." *Audubon*, September–October 2005, 58–62, 72–73.

Silberglied, Robert E. "Visual Communication and Sexual Selection Among Butterflies." In *The Biology of Butterflies*, edited by R. I. Vane-Wright and P. R. Ackery, 207–223. London: Academic Press, 1984.

Simon, Hilda. *Milkweed Butterflies: Monarchs, Models, and Mimics*. New York: Vanguard Press, 1969.

Smart, Paul. *The Illustrated Encyclopedia of the Butterfly World in Color*. Northbrook, IL: Quality Books, 1981.

Smith, David S., Lee D. Miller, and Jacqueline Y. Miller. *The Butterflies of the West Indies and South Florida*. New York: Oxford University Press, 1994.

Steinbeck, John. "Hooptedoodle (2), or The Pacific Grove Butterfly Festival," in *Sweet Thursday*, 246–249. 1954. Reprint, New York: Penguin, 1996.

Stradling, D. J. "The Nature of the Mimetic Patterns of the Brassolid Genera, *Caligo* and *Eryphanis*." *Ecological Entomology* 1 (1976): 135–138.

"Study supports new mass extinction theory." CNN.com. March 18, 2004.

Tampion, John, and Maureen Tampion. *The Living Tropical Greenhouse: Creating a Haven for Butterflies*. Lewes, East Sussex, England: Guild of Master Craftsman Publications, 1999.

Taylor, Chip. "Can Monarchs Detect Sound or Do They Live in a Silent World?" Monarch Watch Update, www.MonarchWatch.org, December 16, 2002.

Taylor, Ronald L. *Butterflies in My Stomach, or: Insects in Human Nutrition*. Santa Barbara, CA: Woodbridge Press, 1975.

Teale, Edwin Way. *Near Horizons: The Story of an Insect Garden*. New York: Dodd, Mead, 1942.

———. *The Strange Lives of Familiar Insects*. New York: Dodd, Mead, 1962.

Tilden, J. W., and Arthur C. Smith. *Field Guide to Western Butterflies*. Peterson Field Guide Series. Boston: Houghton Mifflin, 1986.

Tobin, James. *To Conquer the Air: The Wright Brothers and the Great Race for Flight*. New York: Free Press, 2003.

Tyler, Hamilton A. *The Swallowtail Butterflies of North America*. Healdsburg, CA: Naturegraph Publishers, 1975.

Urquhart, F. A. *The Monarch Butterfly*. Toronto: University of Toronto Press, 1960.

Vane-Wright, R. I., and P. R. Ackery, eds. *The Biology of Butterflies*. London: Academic Press, 1984.

Viegas, Jennifer. "Study: Some Butterflies Talk." *Discovery News*. http://dsc.discovery.com/news/briefs/200040726/butterfly_print.html. July 28, 2004.

Wagner, David. *Caterpillars of Eastern North America*. Princeton, NJ: Princeton University Press, 2005.

Waldbauer, Gilbert. *Millions of Monarchs, Bunches of Beetles*. Cambridge, MA: Harvard University Press, 2000.

———. *What Good are Bugs? Insects in the Web of Life*. Cambridge, MA: Harvard University Press, 2003.

Watson, Allan, and Paul E. S. Whalley. *The Dictionary of Butterflies and Moths in Color*. New York: McGraw-Hill, 1975.

Werner, Alfred, and Josef Bijok. *Butterflies and Moths*. New York: Viking, 1965.

Williams, Ernest, James Adams, and John Snyderl. "FAQ About Butterflies: Size."

Wilson, E. O. *Naturalist*. New York: Warner Books, 1995.

Winterton, Shaun L. "Scales and Setae." In *Encyclopedia of Insects*, edited by Vincent H. Resh and Ring T. Cardé, 1017–1020. San Diego, CA: Academic Press, 2003.

Wootton, Robin J. "Wings." In *Encyclopedia of Insects*, edited by Vincent H. Resh and Ring T. Cardé, 1186–1192. San Diego, CA: Academic Press, 2003.

Xerces Society. *Butterfly Gardening: Creating Summer Magic in Your Garden*. San Francisco: Sierra Club Books, 1990.

Yack, Jayne, and Ron Hoy. "Hearing." In *Encyclopedia of Insects*, edited by Vincent H. Resh and Ring T. Cardé, 498–505. San Diego: Academic Press, 2003.

Yack, Jayne, L. Daniel Otero, Jeff W. Dawson, Annemarie Surlykke, and James H. Fullard. "Sound Production and Hearing in the Blue Cracker Butterfly *Hamadryas Feronia* (Lepidoptera, Nymphalidae) from Venezuela." *Journal of Experimental Biology* 203, no. 24 (2000): 3689–3702.

Young, Allen M. *Sarapiqui Chronicle: A Naturalist in Costa Rica*. Washington, DC: Smithsonian Institution Press, 1991.

Zalucki, Myron P., Anthony R. Clarke, and Stephen B. Malcolm. "Ecology and Behavior of First Instar Larval Lepidoptera." *Annual Review of Entomology* 47 (2002): 361–393.

Index

About the Author and Photographer

Author David Badger
Photograph by Ray Wong

David Badger lives in Franklin, Tennessee, with his wife, Sherry, and son, Jeff. He is a professor of journalism at Middle Tennessee State University, where he teaches magazine writing, feature writing, arts reviewing, media writing, and motion picture history. He was a film critic for WPLN-FM Public Radio in Nashville for thirteen years, and a book reviewer and columnist for the *Nashville Tennessean* for seventeen years. He grew up in Wilmette, Illinois, and earned an A.B. degree in English literature from Duke University; M.S.J. degree in editorial journalism from Northwestern University; and Ph.D. in communication from the University of Tennessee.

He is the author of *Frogs* (Voyageur Press, 1995), *Snakes* (Voyageur Press, 1999), *Frogs: WorldLife Library* (Voyageur Press, 2000), and *Lizards: A Natural History of Some Uncommon Creatures—Extraordinary Chameleons, Iguanas, Geckos, & More* (Voyageur Press, 2002), all illustrated with photographs by John Netherton. He is the co-author of *Newscraft*, a contributor to *Free Expression and the American Public*, and the editor of more than a dozen books by John Netherton.

Brian Kenney's spectacular images have won multiple awards in the prestigious National Wildlife and BBC Wildlife Photographer of the Year competitions. By carefully observing his subjects, he is able to anticipate behavior and capture the spirit of the animal on film. His work has appeared in most of the major nature publications, including *Audubon*, *BBC Wildlife*, *Birder's World*, *BrownTrout*, *National Geographic*, *National Wildlife*, *Natural History*, *Outdoor Photographer*, *Ranger Rick*, *Sinra*, *Das Tier*, and *Wildlife Conservation*.

Brian's previous books include *Florida's Fabulous Butterflies* (with Thomas Emmel) and *Florida's Fabulous Insects* (with Mark Deyrup). Each year, hundreds of his photographs appear in books, magazines, and calendars around the world. He shares his home in North Port, Florida, with a gardenful of butterflies.

Photographer Brian Kenney
Photograph by Alfred Gordon

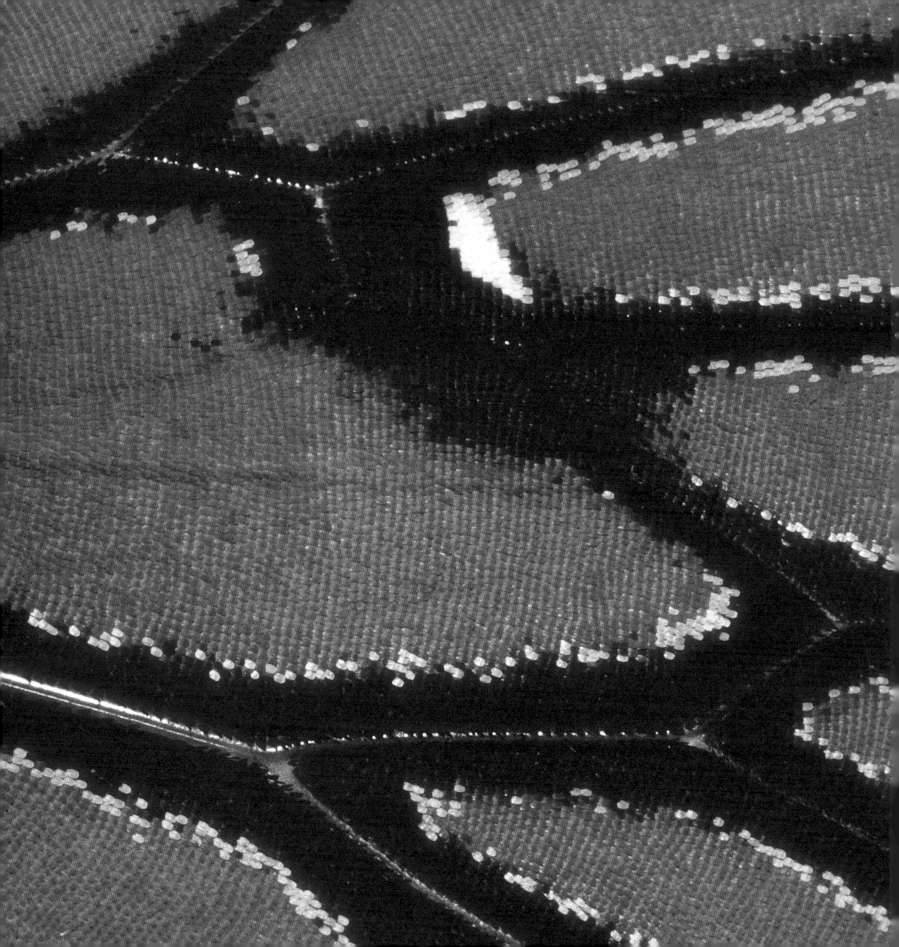